CONTENT

LIST OF PHOTOGRAPHS AND MAPS

MORE MURDER AND MAYHEM
AROUND THE CHASE

Rugeley

Pye Green

Penkridge

Hednesford

High Town

Rawnsley

Cannock

Wimblebury

Hatherton

Chase Terrace

Leacroft

Heath Hayes

Bridgtown

Burntwood

Churchbridge

Norton Canes

Anthony Hunt

Published by
Mount Chase Press
109 Mount Street, Hednesford, Cannock, Staffs. WS12 4DB
01543 422891

ISBN 978-0-9551382-3-2

Designed and produced by John Griffiths

ACKNOWLEDGEMENTS

Once again may I thank all the staff of the libraries, especially those at Cannock, who have suffered my constant badgering for information, old maps and Census Returns whilst producing this book. Your patience is much appreciated.

Also many thanks to those people and local history societies who have kindly loaned the following pictures:- D. Battersby for 23 & 28; S. Belcher for 6, 35 & 36; Birmingham Post for 27; R. Bradbury for 25, 26 & 46; Bridgtown Historical Society for 47; M. Cartwright for 4; Cheslyn Hay Local History Society for 1; T. Dudley for 31; M. Gray for 19 & 22; R. Knowles for 33; E. Morgan for 41; J. Pickerill for 21; R. Smith & Museum of Cannock Chase for 17, 20, 30 & 34; and J. Taylor for 37.

Any photographs loaned by the various local history societies and the museum were done so in the good faith that the original owners would be only too pleased to see their photographs in print.

Finally, all the photographs were loaned in good faith, but apologies to anyone whose copyright may have been unintentionally infringed.

INTRODUCTION

Once again I have scoured the local newspapers during the Victorian era and the early twentieth century and have discovered yet another series of crimes from our local towns and villages. Added to these I have decided to include some cases not strictly within the boundaries of Cannock Chase, like Rugeley and Penkridge, simply because I include them in various talks I give to local societies and I thought it was about time I wrote about them also.

What may astound you is that I managed to locate so many more cases in our small area without including much more recent crimes. It just goes to prove that our day and age is not quite as violent as we are led to believe compared with that of our ancestors. Newspapers and television would have us believe that we are in danger at almost every turn, even in our own homes. What we have to remember always is that bad news sells more papers and gruesome reports on television invariably get more viewers. Strangely when the BBC tried including a slot of "good" news few viewers tuned in.

But just how evil was the Victorian or Edwardian eras compared with today? Compare the following government statistics and you will discover that in today's world we are far safer than our ancestors.

Murders in 1868
Up to Michaelmas and including England and Wales - 129 murders

Metropolitan District - 13	10.1% (London had more than 10% of the population)
Boroughs - 51	39.5%
Counties – 65	50.4% of those Lancashire had 40 (27 in Liverpool alone)
	Cheshire had 8
	Staffordshire had 7
	Yorkshire had 6
	Gloucestershire had 6

Proportion of murders to the population

1866	**1 in every 161,908 people**
1867	**1 in every 158,737 people**
1868	**1 in every 167,824 people**
1991	**1 in every 261,891 people (201 murders)**
2001	**1 in every 188,516 people (285 murders)**

As for attempted murders the figures are even more revealing.

1866	**?**	**1 in every 345,907 people**
1867	**?**	**1 in every 476,211 people**
1868	**61**	**1 in every 471,333 people**
1991	**56**	**1 in every 940,002 people**
2001	**48**	**1 in every 1,119,316 people**

Yet somehow we are still led to believe that we are living in a much more dangerous society than our ancestors. The media has a lot to answer for.

Another myth that needs to be challenged is that Victorian courts were extremely strict and severe with criminals. What may surprise you in this book is the lack of cases where the death penalty was the outcome. It would seem that Victorian courts were far more understanding than we might give them credit for and were far more willing to show mercy. By the mid nineteenth century gone were the eighteenth century attitudes to crime where there were scores of offences for which the death penalty was the only answer, like sheep stealing and burglary, and they were replaced by a more reasoned era of punishment. Figures again from 1868 go some way to prove that.

Number of Apprehensions for Murder in 1868

118 of which **99** were committed to trial – **74** men and **25** women. By the end of that year **71** of them were committed to trail of which **38** were acquitted; **12** found to be insane; and **21** convicted and given the death sentence (**17** men and **4** women).

Of those **21** people given the death sentence **1** was pardoned; **6** men and **2** women were given penal servitude for life, which might include transportation; and only **10** men and **2** women were executed.

Since the capital sentence had been restricted to murder in **1861** there had been an average of 29 convictions per year with only **14** of those being executed.

In this book you will see that some possible death sentences were replaced by transportation to the colonies like Australia or Canada or replaced by life imprisonment. Victorian court decisions were no longer "black or white", but extenuating circumstances were being taken into account more and more. They were heading towards a more sensible and civilised system of justice which would eventually lead to the abolition of the death penalty. But I leave you, the reader, to argue the pros and cons of that decision.

However, there was one crime which the Victorians never really understood, that of suicide, as an article in the *Cannock Advertiser,* dated July 1887, would suggest. The reporter wrote, "Whence comes this epidemic of suicides? Recent discussions have named several causes. One writer suggests it to infidel teachings, holding that hopelessness of a future state cripples fortitude for bearing life's ill; another declares suffering from the universal business depression the cause; a third attributes it to increasing insanity; a physician thinks much of the tendency is inherited; while the temperance advocates lay the responsibility upon strong drink. Well nigh every report of suicide and family murder mentions the perpetrator as having for some time been subject to melancholy."

You will find several cases of suicide in this book and learn that Victorian courts were trying desperately to understand the victims. Greater emphasis was being placed on the psychological aspects of the crime and so those cases, once thought to be such dreadful offences to God that churches would not allow burials within their grounds, were examined more carefully and the victim pitied rather than punished. Also around that time institutions for those affected by melancholy were gradually changing (though at a slower rate) with treatment at the fore rather than just being used as a "dumping ground for the insane".

The confines or rules of law are slow to change, but often ordinary men and women, acting as the jury, began to question those laws and in some cases actually brought about change. Here you will see evidence of the jury questioning points of law and in some cases judges or coroners exasperated by the confines of law. That is very clear in the cases of suicide.

Finally, when reading the various cases ask yourself the questions, "Are my own views on the eventual court decisions more early Victorian than modern? What verdict would I have given?" You may be pleasantly surprised or possibly alarmed at your answer.

ROBBERY WITH INTENT
Hatherton - Rawnsley - Hightown

The dictionary definition of robbery is the act of "violently or feloniously despoiling (damaging) a person, place or property to deprive or cheat someone of their rightful belongings". It is the possibility of violence or even death to the victim, because they will in most cases fight back to stop being robbed, which makes the crime so serious. Victorian law makers considered it almost as bad as actual murder and so sentences were harsh.

The first case in this chapter shows to what "stupid" lengths some criminals will go just to get their hands on other people's property. Fortunately for the victim in this case he narrowly escaped death by putting his own life in danger. Weston Turner, aged around 65, and his wife, Mary aged about 70, kept the Red Lion in Hatherton Parish (on the site of the Roman Way today). As was their usual practise after closing up the pair retired to bed, leaving the bedroom door ajar to enable them to hear the clock downstairs and keep a parental eye on the two girls who lived there. One was

1. Rear of the Red Lion Inn, Wedges Mill.

their daughter, Jane, and the other the serving girl, Anne Dawton. Henry Ganettly, an agricultural labourer employed by Weston, slept in a nearby outhouse.

Sometime during the night Weston was awoken by a door being opened and, thinking it was one of the girls, he called out. Suddenly he was attacked and beaten about the head severely. Somehow he managed to evade his attacker and jumped for his life out of the bedroom window, some fifteen feet above ground level, risking death or at least severe injury. As he landed he heard his wife scream out and then the two attackers raced from the property, but not before stealing some silver, a gun and several other articles.

It was at that point that the "stupidity" of the crime became apparent because Weston recognised one of his attackers. It was none other than John Lovatt, a 26 year old labourer who had lived in the parish of Hatherton and whom Weston had known since Lovatt's childhood. (In the 1841 Census his mother, Sarah, and brother, William, still lived and worked in the Wedges Mill area, but I could find no record of John in that Census.) His accomplice turned out to be 22 year old John Spencer from Hednesford. (In the 1841 Census John Spencer lived with his father, also John, and sister, Anne, at Littleworth Cottage, Hednesford. The family were relatively well off and had moved into Hednesford from St. Georges, Middlesex sometime in the 1830's. None of the family needed to work and lived off the father's fortune, possibly made from horse racing. It, therefore, begs the question as to why John Spencer, junior, needed to steal.)

Because of Weston's positive identification of one of his attackers it was not long before the local constables managed to track down the perpetrators and have them safely locked up to await trial. After the preliminary court appearances before magistrates the pair were sent to Stafford Gaol where they remained until the Assize Court met. On Thursday, March 17th, 1842 the two men were brought before Lord Justice Cresswell and indicted for breaking into the house of Weston Turner on October 12th, 1841 at night and then and there assaulting, cutting and wounding with intent to murder the said Weston Turner and his wife, Mary, and stealing from that house six silver teaspoons, a gun and various articles.

Mr. Turner stated that on the evening of October 11th, 1841 he and his wife retired to bed around 10.30 p.m. Before they went he saw the house safe, checking that the doors and windows were all locked. As was their custom they usually left their bedroom door open a little to hear the downstairs clock and call the girls, his daughter and the servant, in the morning.

Sometime during the night he was awakened by a door being moved. Thinking it was the girls getting up he shouted out, *"What are you girls getting up so soon for?"* There was no answer and so he pulled aside the bed curtain and saw a man's hand with a lighted match in it. He cried out, *"Who are you? What do you do there?"* and a gruff voice answered, *"Damn your b---- eyes, I'll blow your b-----y brains out!"* The

2

witness got up when the match went out, the door was pushed further open and he received a blow on the upper part of the head with some sharp instrument which cut through his nightcap. The person then said, *"D—m your b----y eyes. I'll knock your b----y head off!"* and then immediately called out, *"Jack, bring up the pistol and balls!"* He struck the witness again on the back of the head and knocked him down. The witness got up and was struck a third time on the head. He got up again, opened the window close by and jumped out onto the ground below, some fifteen feet below. Before he jumped he heard his wife shriek.

Under questioning Weston said that he knew the voice of his attacker well; it was Lovatt. He had known him from an infant and Lovatt had frequently been at his house. He was quite sure that his attacker was Lovatt. He also told the court that he had been attended by the surgeon for some time after the attack and was dangerously ill.

Mary Turner, his wife, confirmed all her husband's evidence and told the court that she had been attacked as well.

William Egerton, a metal worker, who also kept a beer house in Brook Lane, Great Wyrley, told the court that on the evening of October 10th, 1841 the two prisoners were at his house. A man named Whitehouse was present and he had said to Spencer, *"Isn't your name John Spencer?"* to which he did not reply. However, Lovatt had said, *"No, he comes from Sheffield and has been working on the railroad there."* The prisoners then left and walked towards Cannock.

William Parker, gardener for Mr. Gilpin of Longford House, stated that as he lived close by the inn at The Lodge he was called to the Red Lion after the burglary and discovered footsteps of two men under the parlour window where they had got in. He traced them a good mile along the Cannock Road and finally lost them at the entrance to a green lane which led in the direction of Spencer's father's house in Hednesford. (It is quite possible that William Parker was the paid parish constable for the area at the time as there was no regular police force set up in the Cannock area at that early date. The Stafford Borough Police Force was only set up in 1840 with one superintendent, one sergeant and two constables for the whole of that town.)

The next witness was John Lockley of 9 Walsall Road, Great Wyrley. He had known Lovatt for many years and on the morning of the robbery, between 7 and 8 o'clock, he had met Lovatt and another person at Churchbridge. Lovatt had a gun on him and his pockets "stood out".

Thomas Williams found a handkerchief containing six table spoons concealed in a bank between Rushall and Pelsall on October 13th. Humphrey Williams, his brother, told the court that he had seen the prisoners not far from that place on the same day.

Jane Bradbury of Littleworth, Hednesford, where Spencer's father lived, said that she was at Spencer's house one day after the crime. When she arrived the door was

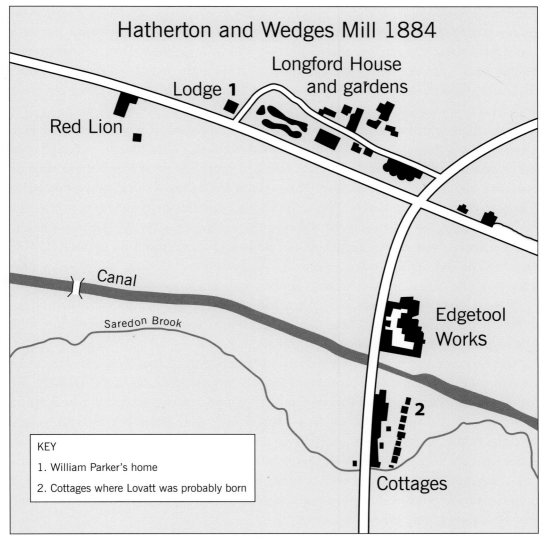

2. Map of Hatherton and Wedges Mill (1884).

fastened, but presently opened by Spencer's sister, Anne. While she was there John Spencer came into the house and said, *"I am afraid they are going to take me for the robbery. They suspect me and John Lovatt and I'll be damned if I must not be off or they will hang or transport me for I've such a hell of a character."* His sister then told him what she had heard of the crime and he replied, *"By God that will do me."*

Isaac Webb, a stone mason living at Erdington, Birmingham, told the court that on October 17th Lovatt came into the Erdington Arms and sat down near him. The prisoner was calling himself Holland and so Isaac had asked him if he was speaking of Dr. Holland of Cannock and the prisoner said that he was. He then began talking with the prisoner and asked him if he had a brother who was a policeman at Cannock. He replied that he had and immediately asked, *"Do you know me?"* The witness then said that he did to which the prisoner replied, *"If you had owned me on the road I should have floored you into a ditch as I did the other man the other night for there is £10 reward offered for me."* The witness then told him that he was neither policeman nor constable and said, "I am not going to take you." The prisoner then said, *"You cannot. There is but three or four of you and I would sweep the b----y set of you."*

Isaac then told the court that he said, *"The constables of Walsall are after you, Raymond and Foxall,"* to which the prisoner replied, *"That little b---- Foxall shall never take me. I shall stab him first."* He then went on to say that there was no evidence against him *"except that old b---- who would say that he struck him as he was getting out of the window"*. When the witness said that he could be transported if he were caught, the prisoner said, *"I was not there, but six miles off."* He also told the witness that he was off to Lancashire, but he would give himself up in the following March as he did not like to be in prison long before the Assizes. The prisoner then left the public house and the witness got two policemen to go after him.

Police Constables Thomas Hutler and John Pearson said that they arrested Lovatt at Sutton Coldfield. He told them that his name was John Cartwright, but they took him to the station where Police Superintendent Foxall received him into custody.

The final witness was Mr. Thomas Holmes, surgeon of Cannock. He stated that he was called to attend Mr. Turner and his wife on the morning of the robbery. He found that Mr. Turner's head had one incised wound and two lacerated wounds and there was other bruising. He was in a "dangerous" state. There was also an incised wound on Mrs. Turner's head, but her wound was not dangerous. As far as he was concerned the incised wounds had been inflicted with a sharp instrument while the other wounds were inflicted with a blunt instrument. Mr. Turner's shirt and their nightcaps were produced in court and were covered in blood. Mr. Holmes presumed that both people had bled profusely.

Lovatt and Spencer had their own Counsels for the Defence. Mr. Yardley, acting for Lovatt, argued that his client had never been seen during the robbery, only a voice heard and Mr. Turner could have been mistaken in the heat of the moment. He also said that at no time had his client tried to sell any of the stolen goods because he did not commit the crime. Mr. Allen, acting for Spencer, said that there was no evidence given during the trial of his client breaking into the Red Lion. The only reason he had been arrested was because he had been seen with Lovatt some time before and after the robbery.

The judge, Lord Justice Cresswell, having summed up, left it to the jury to decide. For half an hour they consulted whilst still in the jury box and then they were taken from the court. After a further hour of discussion they returned to give their verdict. John Lovatt was found GUILTY of robbery with assault, but NOT with intent to murder. John Spencer was found NOT GUILTY of any crime and so ACQUITTED.

Before he passed sentence the following day Lord Justice Cresswell asked Lovatt if he had anything to say as to why he should not receive the sentence of death. Lovatt simply answered, *"I am innocent."* The judge then proceeded to address Lovatt as follows, *"I have not the least doubt of your guilt and my impression at first was that it would have been my painful duty to have passed on you the awful sentence of death and left you for execution. But I have most unctuously reconsidered your case and, as the jury negated that part of the indictment which charged you with intent to murder, I shall recommend that your life be spared and you be sentenced to TRANSPORTATION FOR LIFE."* Lovatt was led from the court to await his fate.

* Transportation to the colonies was finally ended in the 1850's, but by that time thousands of men, women and even children had been sent, some for the most meagre of crimes.

* Spencer returned home to Hednesford the day before Lovatt was sentenced, but he disappeared from Hednesford soon after along with his father. Anne, his sister, stayed and married George Whitehouse, the jockey, and they continued to live in Littleworth Cottage for many years. By the time of the 1851 Census Weston Turner and his wife, Mary, had presumably died, and their daughter, Jane, was keeping the Red Lion.

Most robberies are well planned to avoid the need for violence. Lovatt was just "unlucky" that his victim woke up and disturbed him, but what of the robber who deliberately sets out knowing that he will have to inflict harm on his victim? The following is just such a case where the serial offender had used violence in the past.

On Saturday, October 13th, 1877 William Watkins, a groom for Mr. Williamson, the manager of Cannock and Rugeley Colliery at Rawnsley, was driving his master's dog cart as usual from Hednesford to Cannock Wood, having collected the money from a Hednesford bank to pay the wages of the workers at the colliery. As he neared the colliery tramway which ran from the railway to the pit he was suddenly attacked by a man who had been lying in wait. His assailant made a dash for the cart and, banging on the cart with one hand, beat Mr. Watkins about the head with a loaded stick (a piece of wood with metal imbedded). Watkins was smothered in blood and knocked almost insensible, but he had sufficient strength to whip the horse forward and his attacker, realising he had failed, made his escape. What the attacker had failed to realise was that Watkins was not carrying the wages as presumed, but had dropped the bags off at the Valley Colliery Offices to be collected later.

Having made his way back to Mr. Williamson's offices at the Grange (on the map as Cannockwood House) Watkins was then taken home where he was attended by Dr. Cooper. He remained in a dangerous state for two months, but finally recovered. His assailant meanwhile had fled and nothing more was heard of him in the area for over two years. It would only be his own self-confidence that would eventually let him down.

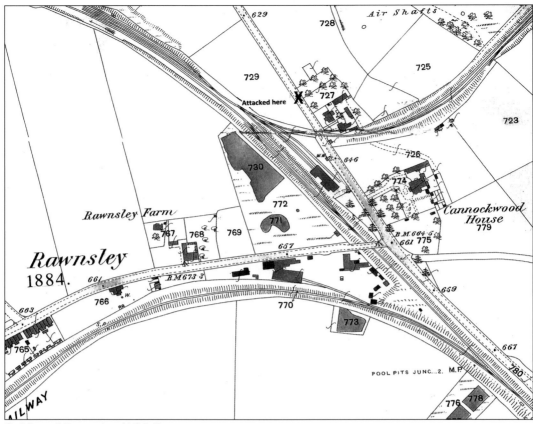

3. Map of Rawnsley (1884).

On Friday, January 18th, 1878 a warehouse porter named William Cook was standing in Aberdeen Street, Birmingham near Winson Green Prison and was accosted by one Simeon Bird aged 24 who assumed that Cook had recently been in gaol. After some conversation Bird told Cook that he had a "job" for a man who had recently been in gaol and the proceeds would keep him for two or three years without work. Cook then consented to helping Bird with his plan which was to rob a Mr. Peter Poncia's house in Cleveland Road, Balsall Heath. Apparently the old man had a lot of money left him which he kept at home.

Convinced that he had found an accomplice Bird left, but Cook went immediately to the detective office at Moore Street and told Detective Sergeant Black the story. Acting on Black's instructions Cook kept up his communications with Bird and the two became closer. After several meetings Bird became even more communicative and told Cook all about the "little affair" he had had at Hednesford where he had knocked a man about who had been to the bank for £800 with which to pay the men who were employed at a colliery. He told Cook that he had worked in Hednesford for a short while and had got to know of the wages delivery through local gossip. He also informed Cook that if they were successful in the robbery at Mr. Poncia's home then he planned another at a house in Duchess Road, Edgbaston where there was a lot of money. He knew that because his girl lived there.

Terms were arranged as to Cook's share of the booty and on Friday, January 25th, 1878 the two men went to Mr. Poncia's home. Bird was at once seized by Black and two constables. In one hand he had a fictitious note for Mr. Poncia and in the other a life-preserver, whilst in his trouser pocket was a six chambered loaded revolver and some leather straps which he afterwards said he had intended using to fasten Mr. Poncia's legs while he robbed the house.

Bird was tried at the Worcester Quarter Sessions for inciting Cook to commit a felony and given a two year sentence. On completion of his gaol term he was immediately arrested by Sergeant Cockerell of Cannock and taken to Stafford. On Monday, March 15th, 1880 Simeon Bird appeared before the magistrates, the Hon. E.G.P. Littleton and Messrs. B. Gilpin and R.H. Briscoe, at Cannock.

William Watkins told of the vicious attack he had undergone on October 13th 1877 and how he had probably been saved from a worse fate by the tall hat which he wore which took the heaviest blows and by the appearance of a man walking up the road. He told the hearing that he was confined to his bed on account of his injuries and had been unable to do anything for ten weeks. He also informed the hearing that he had noticed the defendant on previous journeys near the same spot where he was attacked.

Dr. G.B. Cooper testified that he had tended Watkins on the day of the attack and afterwards. He had received two severe wounds on the head, one on the right side and one on the top. He had lost a considerable amount of blood and for some time the doctor felt Watkins was in a critical condition. William Cook and Detective Sergeant Black also gave evidence as to the whereabouts of Bird over the last few years and facts as to his character. With little hesitation the magistrates committed Bird to appear at the next Assizes.

In April, 1880 Simeon Bird, a draper's assistant formerly of Birmingham, stood trial and was indicted for *"feloniously wounding William Watkins with intent to maim, disfigure or disable him"*. His wretched criminal history was related to the court and finally he was asked to make a statement. He pleaded not guilty to the attack and made a long rambling statement to the effect that he knew nothing about the charge and that on the day he was alleged to have attacked Watkins he was in Birmingham. He also argued that his two years' imprisonment was sufficient for anything that he had done and he smilingly informed the jury that the Government would not make any profit out of him if he was sentenced to a further term of imprisonment as he was too delicate to do much manual labour.

The jury were not convinced and found Bird GUILTY. His Lordship in addressing Bird said that he had been justly convicted of a most daring crime committed in broad daylight and was fortunate not to kill the man. Because he had shown what a daring and desperate character he was and because of the dreadful history he had displayed the judge had to protect the public from such a man. He therefore sentenced Bird to fifteen years penal servitude. Bird, who seemed confused and surprised at the severity of the sentence, was immediately taken from the dock.

The final case in this chapter is what is defined as an opportunistic robbery – mobile phones get snatched from victims, purses are taken from bags or money left lying around is lifted. There is no forward planning as the victim is not known to the perpetrators, merely presents himself/herself in the wrong place at the wrong time. To avoid such nightmares people are advised by the police, or television today, not to "advertise" their wealth and where possible avoid unsafe situations. That is just the very advice that William Sheldon of Dudley should have followed in June, 1896. Not only was he in the notoriously rough area at the time of Hightown drinking late at night, but he had boasted of the money he had about his person.

> ** Hightown had sprung up in the late 1870's due to the opening up of the coal mines in the area and was comprised largely of mining families from the Black Country, itself a rather "rough" place with a legacy of violent crimes.*

William Sheldon was a hawker by trade and lived at Prospect Row, Dudley with his wife and children. On Friday, June 5th, 1896 he went to a friend's house in Hightown and stayed the night. On the Saturday he remained in Hednesford and visited other people whom he knew from his days as a hop-picker employer. Those friends lived in Bradford Street and when he left he went into a public house (possibly the Rising Sun on the corner of Bradford Street) to have a drink while he waited for his train. There he got talking to a group of men he had not met before and stupidly made it known that he had quite a lot of money hidden in his shoes. What was even more ludicrous was that he accompanied some of them back to a house for more drink, missing his train and later to be robbed in a violent manner by those very men. Had it not been for the timely intervention of a woman shouting from her bedroom window that robbery could have turned to murder.

On Monday June 8th two men had been arrested for the crime and appeared before Cannock Petty Sessions. They were brothers Charles (Chas) Stokes, aged 23, and James Stokes, aged 18, of Bradford Street. Both were remanded to appear before the magistrates at Penkridge the following week. (In those days the magistrates held their courts in Penkridge and Cannock in turn.) After the hearing James Stokes made a statement to Sergeant Burgess in consequence of which the sergeant and Police Constable Taylor arrested John Cooksey on the Wednesday afternoon at one o'clock. At the same time John Hadlington was also arrested. They were taken before Mr. Wolverton at Hednesford at four o'clock and remanded in custody until the following Monday and then taken to Hednesford Police Station.

4. Hednesford Police Station around 1910.

The men were placed in separate cells for the night and during that night were visited by various officers as was the custom. Sergeant Burgess saw them at 3.00 a.m. and then Constable Beech saw them three times after before 6.00 a.m. They were then visited the last time at 7.30 a.m. when they were fine. About ten minutes later they heard Cooksey shout to Hadlington and ask him how he was. Hadlington said he could not sleep and was going to tell the police all he knew. About 8.30 a.m. Constable Jeffrey went to take Hadlington his breakfast and then went to Cooksey's cell where he found him hanging by his belt from one of the iron heating pipes. As soon as the constable touched Cooksey the strap broke and the body fell to the floor. He called Burgess immediately and Dr. Phillips was sent for. He pronounced Cooksey "quite dead" adding that, as the body was still warm, he estimated the death at around 8.00 a.m.

> *I have found no investigation of the police procedure as there certainly would have to be today and can only presume that it was just taken for granted that they were in no way to blame for Cooksey's death.*

On Monday June 15th four men, all miners, were brought before the magistrates to answer the charge of robbery with violence. They were the two Stokes brothers from Bradford Street; Edward Fowler, aged 25, who had also been implicated, and John Hadlington, aged 25, who lived at the same address also in Bradford Street.

* John Hadlington had been the captain of Hednesford Town Football Team in the 1884/85 season. It must have been slightly embarrassing for the officials of the club because on Tuesday, June 23rd 1896 they held their Annual General Meeting and, after a successful season where they finished second in the league, they handed out medals to various members of the team. Unfortunately Hadlington, who should have received three medals, was languishing in the Hednesford cells at the time.

The first person to give evidence was William Sheldon. He said that he had been in Hednesford on Friday June 5th and had stayed overnight with friends. At that time he had £18 7s 9d on him and spent just 3s 9d that night. On Saturday June 6th he had visited other friends in Bradford Street and on leaving he had gone into a public house to have a drink while he waited for his train. There he met the prisoners and they had some drink together in two different houses and in a yard. Chas Stokes was with them for about an hour and afterwards they all went into Mrs. Hughes's house and remained there until about midnight. When he left he went out of the front door and said, *"Goodnight."* Chas and James Stokes came down the entry and overtook him and said, *"This is the way to the railway station"* and turned him to the right. As soon as he turned they got hold of him, threw him down and took £3 out of his right boot. They were the only two there at that time. When they threw him down he shouted, *"Police!"* and *"Murder!"* They then allowed him to get up and he ran to a house occupied by a Mrs. Fallows. The house stood in a garden and he jumped over the fence to get there and then he knocked the door three or four times.

Someone came to the window and he told the person that some men had taken two sovereigns and two half sovereigns out of his boot and that they were coming again and would take his other money if they did not let him in. The men came up again and Chas Stokes said that if he said that he had taken his money he would knock his brains out. At that point the person at the window said, *"We don't want you here, you had better go to the Police Station."* He turned and had to walk away with the men. When they got a short distance up the street Cooksey threw him on the ground and knelt on his chest. Again he shouted, *"Police, murder!"*

Sheldon continued and said that he believed that it was Hadlington who put dirt in his mouth to stop him shouting. Hadlngton also had a razor and he threatened to draw it across the witness's throat. He had said, *"I'll do it just now"*, but Fowler shouted, *"Don't do that!"* He remembered that Cooksey and Hadlington were at the front of him with the two Stokes at his back. As he was on the ground Chas Stokes held his legs while Fowler held his head. They pulled off his left boot and either pulled or cut off his stocking foot, leaving the rest of the stocking. Out of that stocking they took ten sovereigns in gold, one half sovereign, one sixpence, one threepenny piece and a five shilling piece. They also took a shilling, two pennies, two half pennies and his knife out of his right hand pocket as well as a sovereign in a white skin purse, ten shillings, a farthing with H on it which he had had for the last ten years. They tore the inside of his jacket and his watch was dragged out and damaged. There were five men there towards the end of the struggle.

When they had finished robbing him they ran away. He chased after them, almost catching hold of Fowler. On his way back to retrieve his boot he met Constable Beech and told him what had happened. Until he met the constable he had not realised that his right eye was cut and was bleeding. The constable took him to see Sergeant Burgess to relate his attack. During the interview he told the sergeant that he had had between five and seven drinks with the men, but he was sure that they had drugged him. He told the magistrates that for days after the attack his throat had been very bad and he had been unable to eat any solid food.

Under questioning from Mr. Evans, one of the magistrates, who was curious to know how the men knew Sheldon had money on him, Sheldon told the hearing that during the evening Hadlington had dressed up in a fancy dress costume and sang various songs. Hadlington was wearing a good pair of brown boots and was asking everyone to admire them. He told Hadlington that he would not exchange

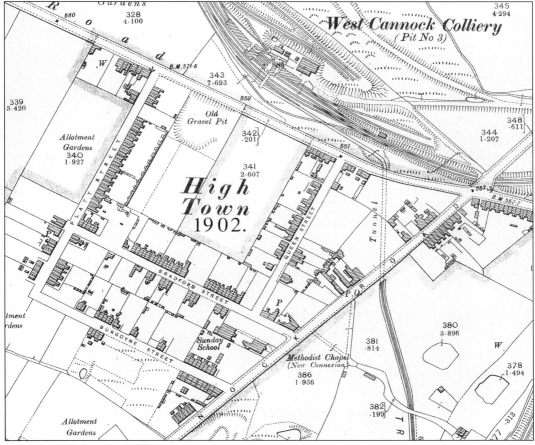

5. Map of Hightown (1902).

his for them and boasted, *"Mine are worth more than yours. I wouldn't take £5 for mine."* He inadvertently must have said that his boots contained his money. Evans then said, *"In fact you practically told them that your money was in your boots?"* and Sheldon had to agree. It would seem that Mr. Evans was blaming Sheldon for the attack. Can victims be blamed for the crime against them?

When asked about the men in the dock who were accused of the attack Sheldon said that there was no mistake about the men. *"They were the ones who had robbed him."* He was interrupted by Chas Stokes who shouted that he was not there and all the other prisoners knew that, *"He had a witness to that effect."*

Police Constable Beech said that he was on duty in Belt Road at 12 o'clock on the evening when he heard shouts of *"Murder!"* and *"Police!"* in the direction of Bradford Street. He went there and discovered a boot and saw Mr. Sheldon who appeared very excited and from every appearance he had been badly used. His mouth was full of dirt and he had a fresh cut over his right eye which was bleeding. One of his stocking feet had been torn or cut off. The man had been drinking and appeared stupefied. He noticed that there had been a struggle where the boot was found. The man then told him that his attackers had taken all the gold out of his boot. At that point he took him to Sergeant Burgess at Hednesford Police Station. At the station he asked for water to wash out his mouth.

Fanny Stokes, mother of the two Stokes lads, said that she was a widow and lived in Bradford Street. She first said that saw the prosecutor (Sheldon) go out of Mrs. Hughes's house by the front door as she was in the kitchen (impossible because the design of those terraced houses had the kitchen by the back door), but later changed her mind about being in the kitchen. She then said that she saw Hadlington and Cooksey go out of the back and go in the direction taken by Sheldon. She had heard Hadlington say he would clean Sheldon out.

At that point Hadlington interrupted and asked how she could say that when he was with her son all night. However, Mrs. Stokes said that she was quite sure that Hadlington was with Cooksey. She told the hearing that Mrs. Hadlington was present when her husband claimed to know nothing about the affair and then overheard Mrs. Hadlington say that her husband was *"up to his tricks"*. The witness insisted that Chas Stokes was not with them and said that she hoped the Lord would strike her dead if she was not telling the truth.

In an attempt to clarify the situation Mr. Simkin, the Clerk, asked exactly who was in the Hughes' house that evening. Mrs. Stokes replied, *"Beside Sheldon, there was Hadlington, Cooksey and his wife, Joseph Hadlington's wife, Edward Fowler, Oliva Gosling, Charles Stokes, Rebecca Gosling, a lodger, John Hughes, his wife and children."* Mr. Simkin asked what they were all doing there at midnight, but Mrs. Stokes never really answered him only saying that she was only in and out during the evening some three times.

Continuing she said that at 10.30 p.m. Chas Stokes sent for a half gallon of beer. She was there at 10 p.m. when Sheldon was there saying that he had lost two half sovereigns. She went in again at 11.30 p.m. because she saw Charlotte Cooksey there. Sheldon mentioned the lost money again and turned to Cooksey and said that he believed him to have it. Cooksey replied that if he said so again he would knock him through the wall. Mrs. Cooksey got a candle to see if Sheldon's boot was unfastened and remarked that the boots had elastic fasteners. She then went to search her husband's pockets, but he would not let her and threatened to knock her down. Hadlington then took hold of Cooksey by the neck and put him out into the back yard. Chas Stokes then said to Sheldon, *"Well, where you have lost your money you go again. I am master here while he* (meaning Mr. Hughes) *is in bed."* Mrs. Stokes then told the hearing that she had said to Sheldon, *"If I were you I would go home, if you have one to go to."* He replied that he had a wife and children at home. At that point they all left the house except Mrs. Hughes and the children, Rebecca Gosling and Chas Stokes.

She then said that as Sheldon was going towards the front door she said to Mrs. Hughes, *"Open the door, Mrs. Hughes, and let the man go."* He left and the door was locked behind him. Chas Stokes stayed there with his young woman. The witness then said that she went to the bottom of the entry and saw Mrs. Hadlington sitting on her doorstep and she said to the witness, *"I wish you had been a little sooner. That man has been saying he has lost £6."* While they were there Hadlington and Cooksey came down the street.

Questioned by Mr. Evans as to when she heard Hadlington say he would have the money she said she heard him say so several times. Once was in the afternoon when Sheldon was showing his boots. He said he had £6 in one and something in the

6. Backs of houses in Bradford Street, Hightown.

other and the boys were betting with him as to how much they contained. Under further questions she said that she first saw Sheldon at 7.30 a.m. on the Saturday and then at 2.30 p.m. in the afternoon. He was also at Knowles's house. It was Joseph's Hadlington's wife who brought him to the house when he really wanted to go home at 5.00 p.m.

Sergeant Burgess gave evidence as to the arrest of Stokes and then of Hadlington who stated that he had never seen the man, but afterwards said that he did not see why he should have all the blame and made a statement. He said that Cooksey was the man who took the money from Sheldon. That was at 11 o'clock on the Sunday. At 12 o'clock he arrested Edward Fowler. Police Constable Taylor had accompanied him and on his arrest Mrs. Sarah Fowler had said, *"Don't you do anything at yourself, never mind if you get twelve ----- months."* James Stokes was also arrested and he made a statement to the effect that James Cooksey and Hadlington followed Sheldon and took the money from him out of his boot. He heard the shouts of *"Murder!"* and *"Police!"* and went into the house. Some of the money was taken from Sheldon in Knowles's house. (Richard Knowles, a miner, lodged with the Fowlers in Bradford Street.) Nine of them had 2s 6d each.

Constable Taylor corroborated Sergeant Burgess's evidence and added that footprints were traced from the top of Bradford Street to where Sheldon was robbed. He also said that he had asked Hadlington if he had a razor. He had denied having one, but later one was found on his mantelpiece. Chas Stokes stated that he was not with the men and urged his brother to say what he knew about the affair.

Rebecca Gosling, a single woman who lived with the Hughes family, stated that she was engaged to Chas Stokes and already had two illegitimate children by him. She saw Chas at Hughes's on the night in question. He came between 10 and 10.30 p.m. and stayed all night until 3 or 4 in the morning. She saw Sheldon there, but he did not stop more than ten minutes. None of the prisoners were there then. She overheard a conversation about £2 being missing and heard Sheldon say that he thought Cooksey had taken it. Cooksey's wife said he had not got the money and turned her husband's pockets inside out. Sheldon went through the front door and the others by way of the back door. Chas Stokes did not leave with them.

At that point the magistrates ended the hearing and refused bail to all of the men, including Chas Stokes. They were all remanded until the following Monday. I think that the magistrates, like me, were so unhappy and confused with the conflicting statements that they hoped matters would be made clearer by the time of the next hearing. One often hears about the solidarity of the criminal fraternity, but here it seemed that every man would "rat" on his friends just to escape justice himself.

On Monday June 22nd all four men were brought before the magistrates at Cannock Police Court. All the evidence having been read again from the hearing at Penkridge several new witnesses were called.

Mary Fallows of Hightown said that on the night of the robbery she had heard someone knocking at her door about midnight. On going to the window a man said they had run him down and robbed him and asked to be let in. As he was speaking a man came up and said he would find him lodgings, but the man (Sheldon) said, *"Go away. I have had enough of you."* He said they had taken two half sovereigns from him. Another man then came up and they all went down Bradford Street. A short time after she heard a man shouting *"Murder!"* She recognised some of the men in the dock as those men at her house.

Eliza Hill, wife of Thomas Hill of Platt Street, said that at 12.30 a.m. on the night she was in bed and heard cries of *"Murder!"* She got up and saw three men standing at the corner of Bradford Street and three other men struggling. One of the men said, *"Hit him,"* and then they disappeared.

Mary Ann Jackson, wife of William Jackson of Platt's Buildings, said that she also heard the shouts and got up from bed. She saw two or three men standing at the shop corner of Bradford Street. She opened the window and saw that two or three other men had got a man down. She shouted, *"What are you doing?"* and they ran away. Altogether she saw five or six men.

Rachael Hadlington, aged twelve, said that she lived with her parents in Bradford Street and her uncle John gave her half a sovereign and sent her for a quarter of bacon. Her uncle lived with them and he had not done any work for five or six months.

Sarah Ann Craddock, wife of Joseph Craddock a miner, said that she ran a money club from her house. (Like Christmas Clubs that are still run today to save for the event.) Mrs. Hadlington was a member of the club and some eight weeks ago she paid her ten shillings, which was her draw, as she was short of money.

Emma Hughes, wife of John Hughes, in whose house Sheldon stayed until midnight gave the names of those in her house that night. Her husband was in bed. Chas Stokes was lying on the sofa and sent for some beer. Sheldon came in and said to Cooksey, *"You look like the man who took my boot off and stole my money."* Cooksey's wife turned his pockets out and there was nothing in them. Sheldon was drunk and so she told him to go and lie down where he had got drunk as he was not going to stay in her house. He then left through the front door.

When questioned by Sergeant Burgess she had said that she had gone to bed at about twelve o'clock. She knew that Chas Stokes did not go out because she was awake and did not hear the door being unlocked.

Mr. R.A. Wilcock, who had been engaged on behalf of Hadlington and Fowler, had to admit that there was a prima facie case against his clients and that there was no doubt that they would have to face trial at the Assizes, but asked for bail. Mr. E. Loxton, solicitor for the two Stokes lads, also applied for bail. The magistrates, after advice from the Clerk, agreed bail for Chas Stokes of £40 and two sureties of £20. However, they could not agree to bail for the other three. All four would appear at the next Assizes in July.

When the case opened on July 22nd Mr. M. Brown for the Prosecution brought forward all the witnesses from the magistrates' hearings and each retold their stories without any new evidence being put forward. All the Defence could offer was that their clients insisted that when the offence was committed they were at home. It did not take the jury long to find the prisoners GUILTY with the exception of Chas Stokes who was ACQUITTED. James Stokes was given four months in gaol; Edward Fowler received five months; and John Hadlington six months.

> *Less than a year later in March, 1897 John Henry Fowler, aged 21, of Bradford Street, a younger brother of Edward Fowler, was involved in the death of Catherine Dooley and was given three years penal servitude. That episode is retold in Murder & Manslaughter around Cannock Chase also by Anthony Hunt.*

I am not sure whether Chas Stokes ever married Rebecca Gosling as the 1901 Census has him lodging with Daniel Moore and his family, but still in Bradford Street. The *1914 Blue Book* does have a C. Stokes occupying 14 Bradford Street as the head of the household, but unfortunately the book only records the head of house, rather like today's Telephone Directories.

Unlike today's footballers whose transgressions are forgiven, it would appear that Hednesford Town Football Club no longer required the services of John Hadlington as he did not appear in their 1897/98 team.

MONEY - THE ROOT OF ALL EVIL
Rugeley

I have been taught to believe that all men are by nature inheritantly good, but occasionally their upbringing, social conditions or tragedies in life may just taint that quality. However, when I research some people's stories my faith in human nature can be severely tested and I just wonder if some individuals are born naturally evil. Hitler may immediately spring to mind, but we have an example in our area – William Palmer.

William was born in today's Station Road, Rugeley on October 24th, 1824, the seventh child of Sarah and Joseph Palmer (they were to have another son, Thomas, later). They owned a large house called "The Yard" which still stands today, opposite St. Augustine's Church. Joseph Palmer had made his fortune buying and selling timber from the Paget Beaudesert Estate and that of the Bagot family at Abbots Bromley. The Napoleonic Wars had seen an increasing need for good timber for the rebuilding of the English Navy and Joseph had cashed in on the demand. (It was rumoured that Mrs. Palmer had used her feminine wiles on the Paget estate manager to gain the contract.)

7. "The Yard" Palmer's birthplace.

8. Old St. Augustine's Church, Rugeley.

From the beginning Sarah doted on her son, William, probably the cause of his wayward behaviour. He was always forgiven. Right from an early childhood he had developed a longing for money (not his own) and frequently borrowed money from his father's workmen which his mother paid back if she found out. As he grew up he was sent to Rugeley Free Grammar School just up the road from his home and again he was found to borrow money, that time from the other boys, and once again mother paid it back. At the age of twelve his father died suddenly. Apparently the family had just finished an evening meal of bread and cheese and Joseph collapsed and died. In his will he left each of the boys a sum of £7,000, equivalent to almost half a million in today's money.

In 1841, at the age of seventeen, William finished his education at the Grammar School and his mother found him a position with Evans and Sons, a Liverpool wholesale chemists business. They bought in chemicals and then sold them to doctors and smaller shops throughout the north of England and the Midlands. He was also found lodgings with a Mrs. Widnall, a respectable widow, and her daughter, Jane. Once away from home and the clutches of his doting mother, William began to develop his two other favourite pastimes – gambling and women. Surrounded by many local race courses William began to bet heavily on the races, but he was never very good at picking winners and soon lost money. With Jane he was more successful and their relationship blossomed.

However, the lack of ready money was a difficulty and so William began to appropriate his master's money. When orders for drugs came in the people invariably sent the money as well. William opened the envelopes, one of his jobs, but also began to take money from them and pocket it. It soon became clear to Mr. Evans that the accounts were not tallying and so he laid a trap. William was caught red-handed. Mr. Evans was all for reporting him to the local constabulary, but Mrs. Palmer intervened. She travelled all the way to Liverpool and persuaded Mr. Evans not to go to the police, but merely sack William. She must have been an excellent talker because, not only did he let William go, but he employed Mrs. Palmer's younger son, Thomas. (It must be said here that Thomas was unlike the rest of the family, he actually became a clergyman in later life.)

William was brought back to Rugeley in some disgrace, but once again mother forgave him and found him another position with Dr. Edward Tylecote of Great Haywood. Aged just eighteen he was to be the doctor's apprentice, able to hand out medicines, though not prescribe them, and deal with minor complaints. Just when everything might have seemed perfect and mother could keep an eye on her son, Mrs. Widnall, who had remarried, and her daughter moved to Great Haywood. A golden opportunity was not to be missed and William renewed his love affair with Jane.

Rumours later had it that the two met secretly while everyone else was at church. In those days anyone who had some social standing had to appear at church just to show how good they were. Apparently William bribed one of the village lads to appear at the church and quite visibly and audibly tell William that he was needed by a sick patient. William would make the most of the fuss and leave – only to appear at Jane's home until the service was over. Their relationship became so serious that the two eloped to Walsall. If that were not enough of a disgrace William had left behind many debts owing to his patients. Mrs. Palmer once again came to the rescue and paid those off while her elder sons went to Walsall and brought the wayward William back home. Incidentally it was never made clear what happened to Jane Widnall.

In 1844, aged just twenty, William was found another position by his mother, that time at Stafford Infirmary. Later that year he went to St. Bartholomew's in London to study medicine. Again out of the family control he wasted his time there on gambling, drinking and women. His lack of effort in his studies became so bad that the hospital authorities wrote to his mother saying that he did not stand a chance of passing his exams. She immediately responded by employing Dr. Stegall, a hospital doctor, to coach William with extra lessons. His pay would be £100 (over £6000 today) after the examinations. Much to everyone's surprise at the hospital William did pass and in 1847 he arrived back at Rugeley to set up practice. Unfortunately Mrs. Palmer had forgotten to pay Dr. Stegall his money and he had to threaten to take her to court. He was finally bought off with just £60.

Once back in Rugeley William set up his practice in Market Street in a house just opposite the Talbot Arms Hotel, but he did not live there. Probably wanting to keep his distance from his mother's overbearing care, he rented a room with Mr. and Mrs. Abley in Little Haywood, a young couple who, because of Mr. Abley's poor health, needed to take in lodgers. It must be made clear here that William was a good doctor and it was not long before he needed to take on an apprentice, Mr. Thirlby, to help in the growing practice. (Competition was not great as the only other doctor available was old Dr. Bamford who was fast approaching his eightieth year.)

9. Site of Palmer's home and surgery, Rugeley.   10. The rear of Palmer's house.

Mr. Abley could possibly be Palmer's first victim. The story had it that the two were drinking one evening with a friend of Palmer at the Lamb and Flag in Little Haywood when Abley was bet that he could not drink two glasses of whisky straight down. Palmer would have been well aware of Abley's poor health and as a doctor he should have known better, unless he had ulterior motives. Stupidly Abley took on the bet and after downing the drinks left the public house only to collapse and die right outside the pub's door. Rumours were rife after his death that Palmer was having an affair with Mrs. Abley.

Those rumours may be totally false because at the same time he had met his future wife. Annie Brookes was the daughter of a retired army officer, Colonel Brookes, and his housekeeper, Mary Thornton. He had made his fortune while serving in India for the East India Company. The British Government had seen fit to send out troops to protect the interests of the Company in India and, what at first started out as purely a trading business, soon developed into colonial aggrandisement with large tracts of India being grabbed by that Company. Officers who went out soon made large sums of money from the Company by helping them to take over areas of the country.

Having retired Colonel Brookes returned to England with his daughter and housekeeper and bought houses in Stafford as an investment. When he died Annie was sent to live with Mr. Dawson, a relative, at Abbots Bromley. There she attended one of the girls' schools and whilst there saw the young, handsome William Palmer who was acting as Dr. Tylecote's assistant and fell in love with him. Apparently William looked after the coughs and colds that the girls caught. She was not to see the young doctor again until he arrived back in the area in 1847, but when they met she fell in love all over again. Their courtship was rapid and the two married in October, 1847 (despite Mr. Dawson's advice) and settled down in Little Haywood.

Mary Thornton did not like Annie's husband and, despite attempts by Annie to persuade her to move in with them at Little Haywood, stayed in Stafford in one of their houses. So much was her dislike of William that she often told stories of how he was trying to kill her; at one point even accusing him of killing her cats. No one would take Mary seriously because unfortunately she was an alcoholic and under the influence often rambled and told incredible tales. However, what is certain is that on Twelfth Night, 1849 Mary was discovered wandering the streets of Stafford in a state of "delirium". Those who found her, afraid that she might die, took her to Annie's home to recover. She never did and died two days later. Had her ramblings about William been true all along?

What is evident is what followed. William persuaded Annie to sell all the houses, but he had not reckoned on Colonel Brookes's will. Brookes knew that Mary was an alcoholic and, afraid that left all the money she might just drink all of the wealth away, he had willed that only the rent from the properties should be given to Mary and Annie on his death and the houses left to another relative, Mr. Shallcross. When Mary died Annie would inherit only those rents. Despite William and Annie contesting the will, the court found in favour of Mr. Shallcross.

Why did William want to get his hands on the money? The young married couple had already started a family, their first son, William Brookes Palmer, being born in 1849. He had also taken up his hobby of gambling again and the doctor's practice was not paying enough to finance that. It was that habit of gambling which led to the death of one of Palmer's associates and probably the first death we can definitely lay at the door of the doctor. During his many visits to the races he became friends with Leonard Bladon, an older gentleman from Ashby de la Zouche, Leicestershire. The two were together once again at Chester Races in May, 1850 and during the five day meeting Leonard was very successful, winning almost a £1,000 once Palmer paid him his betting debts. Elated he wrote to his wife telling her of the good news and also adding that his friend, William Palmer, had invited him to stay with him at Rugeley for a few days.

11. Tombstone of Leonard Bladon's at St. Augustine's.

Leonard never got home. While at Rugeley he fell ill and after several days died of convulsions and vomiting. Palmer himself signed the death certificate despite the possible irregularity. He had already sent for Mrs. Bladon during her husband's illness, but by the time she arrived the funeral and everything had been arranged. As to the £1,000 there was no sign, neither was there any evidence of the betting books which every race-goer kept in those days. Somehow Palmer managed to persuade Mrs. Bladon that Leonard had spent the money and that he had paid her husband the money that he owed him. Amazingly she believed the "good" doctor as he had been so kind to her husband in his last days and returned home. Only years later would she question the events leading to her husband's death.

> ** Betting books were carried by every race-goer in those days as "common" bookies were not allowed on the course. Gentlemen simply gambled between themselves, writing down their bets with friends in their respective books. At the end of a days' racing or at the close of the meeting you simply collected your winnings from your friends or paid them out if you lost. It was the gentleman's code of practice, but as you can see open to skulduggery.*

During the next four years Palmer's financial situation would get progressively worse and all due to the extravagant lifestyle which he could not afford. Determined to be seen as the country gentleman he began not only to continue gambling and be seen at the races, but started to buy his own racehorses, stabling the older ones with William Saunders at Hazel Slade. The yearlings and brood mares he kept at his own stables at Fortesque Lane in Rugeley. He did not buy cheap either; many of the quality horses costing hundreds of pounds. He did manage to have a fair amount of success with them (he won the Chester Cup with Goldfinder in May, 1853 worth well over £2,000), but as anyone who has kept horses will know they are expensive and Palmer was not winning that often to pay for their huge upkeep.

It was during that same time that he most likely killed his own children. After the birth of William, his eldest, he had four more children between 1851 and 1854, but all of them died suddenly within months, weeks or days of being born and all from convulsions. Elizabeth was only ten weeks old; Henry one month; Frank just seven hours; and finally John at four days. The last two were born at the Market Street home (Annie and William had moved there in 1852). On the death of the last child Matilda Bradshaw, their housekeeper, had run screaming from the house and into Bell public house next door ranting to all who would listen that she would not go into the Palmer house again as Palmer was killing his own children. When asked for proof Matilda said that she had been upstairs with baby John when Palmer had come into the room and had said that he would look after the child. She had gone downstairs and suddenly heard the baby screaming. Rushing back up the stairs she found the child dead. She told the people at the pub that she was certain that what Palmer was doing was putting poison on his finger and then covering it with honey and getting the child to suck the finger. However, she had to admit that she had not actually witnessed the act. But she was insistent that Palmer was overheard saying that he could not afford to keep having "all these children" and that he could not altogether blame providence for his children's deaths. When asked again if she had witnessed him doing the dreadful acts she replied, *"No, but I know it in my heart to be true."*

12. Site of the Bell Inn, Rugeley

* Not long ago Kathleen Smith, when writing her dissertation entitled **Sinner, Saint or Political Pawn** *for university, gave another possible cause for the Palmer children's deaths. She stated that it was not unusual for children to die in infancy at that time without any questioning and sometimes families had multiple deaths. She also argued:- "It is also possible that William could have had RH Positive Blood and Annie RH Negative Blood in which case the first born child would live while further pregnancies would be affected by blood poisoning in the womb and after a fifth pregnancy the mother could die." (This was nicknamed Blue Baby Syndrome, but by May 1968 all RH Negative women were injected with Anti D after giving birth to prevent this.)*

Unfortunately to prove this theory the bodies of William and Annie would have to be exhumed and examined. Whilst Annie's still remains in the family grave in St. Augustine's Churchyard in Rugeley William's does not exist as he was buried in Stafford Gaol as you will read later.

If William was limiting his outgoings on the family by getting rid of them he was most certainly not stopping his gambling. In fact the numbers of horses stabled with Saunders at Hazel Slade increased during the same period. He had to look for further income and seems to have turned his attention to his mother's side of the family, all elderly relatives. Perhaps if he endeared himself to them they might just leave him in their wills. But could William wait for them to die?

The first relative he befriended was his uncle Joseph Bentley who himself was a disreputable character, thought to have been involved in arson and robbery. Married three times, it was rumoured that he had killed his second wife by pushing her downstairs. He originally lived in Longdon Green, but moved to Dodsleigh, near Uttoxeter, where he married his third wife. Although distasteful William nevertheless spent time with Joseph, whose third wife had just died, taking him out regularly for drinks. It was after one of their drinking sessions that Joseph died suddenly, in October, 1852. (Rather reminiscent of another drinking session?) Unfortunately no money was left to William and so he sought to comfort another uncle. The second uncle was rich and elderly, but disabled and so looked after by his doting wife. On one visit to Palmer Mrs. Bentley said that she was not feeling too well and so William prescribed tablets for her to take "that very night". Palmer even sent an assistant the next day to see if she had taken the pills. Fortunately she had not and would not but instead threw them outside. Later she was to tell everyone that her chickens ate the pills and promptly died.

It was during this period in English financial history that insurance companies started to extend life insurance policies to greater numbers of the population and unsurprisingly the number of deaths of spouses also began to increase. William was not slow to take up the opportunity of insuring Annie. In April 1854 he persuaded Annie to take out a policy for £13,000 with the Prince of Wales Insurance Company and paid the first premium of £760. It is unclear if his intentions were anything but honourable as he did love Annie, but an opportunity was to come later in the year that he could not refuse.

Annie had gone to Liverpool with Sarah, William's sister, to visit relatives in the September of 1854 and on September 18th she went with Sarah to a concert at Liverpool's St. George's Hall. She wore only a light summer dress that evening and caught a chill. They stayed in Liverpool that evening, but the following day Annie travelled back to Rugeley. On arriving home she was still unwell and so retired to bed. The next morning, Wednesday September 20th, William took her breakfast of tea with sugar but no milk and some dry toast. Soon after she began to vomit. On Sunday September 24th the elderly Dr. Bamford was sent for and he thought it was a case of "English cholera" and prescribed pills containing calomel and colocynth as an "opening drought".

Twice on the Monday another doctor, the near deaf Dr. Knight, and described as "one of the antiquities of Stafford" (he was seventy three years old) also visited Annie, but she was too ill to speak to him. On Tuesday September 26th Dr. Bamford came again to find that only one of his prescribed pills had been taken. That was the last time he would see Annie alive. Palmer's assistant, Dr. Thirlby, also saw Annie and was later to testify that the only medicine he saw Palmer order for Annie was a small dose of prussic acid to reduce the retching.

On Friday, September 29th Palmer wrote in his diary "My poor Annie expired at 10 past 1". Dr. Bamford and Dr. Knight both signed the death certificate giving the cause as English cholera. It was said that Palmer appeared greatly distressed at her funeral held at St. Augustine's Church. It was rumoured at the time that Annie was in very low spirits after the death of her four children and could have brought about her own early demise through grief and worry. However, later events would prove otherwise. An event which probably casts doubt on just how much Palmer loved Annie was the pregnancy of Eliza Tharme, their maid. She gave birth to a son just nine months after Annie's death and it was Palmer's child. Curiously that child also died after five months, but there has never been any suggestion that the infant was murdered.

Having been successful with his insurance claim (he had been fully paid out) it is not difficult to reason that he might just try again because, despite the huge sum of money gained, he was still racking up debts. Try again he did and his next victim would be his brother, Walter, who had fallen into debt and was a serious alcoholic. His drinking habits would surely bring on an early death, but could William cash in before he died and, more importantly, could he find an insurance company to take the risk? Even then insurance companies employed agents to certify that the proposed client was fit.

William settled on a way to get Walter fit enough to pass the medical certificate. He promised Walter £400 if he would stay sober long enough to pass the medical and to insure that he did he employed Tom Walkenden to stay with Walter and make sure that he had no alcohol. Walter agreed to the deal and so William went about getting the insurance policy. After trying at least six different companies he at last managed to find one that would insure Walter for £14,000. No sooner was the policy signed than William gave his brother £60 to do with as he liked, promising the rest later. He also organised unlimited credit for Walter at the local inns. It was like handing candy to a baby; Walter simply drank himself to death by the August of 1855, just as William suspected he would do.

If that was not enough Palmer went off to Liverpool to see Walter's wife. Once there he asked her to repay various debts that Walter was supposed to have incurred. However, he was not to be so lucky because she refused to pay him anything and to make matters worse the insurance company was also refusing to pay out. They could smell a rat and so dispatched two agents to Rugeley to investigate.

For the first time things were not going to plan for Palmer and he still desperately needed extra cash. It was time for a third insurance victim, but who? George Bates was a local farmer who had fallen on hard times. He had had to give up his farm and had found a job with the good doctor Palmer looking after the stables in Fortesque Lane. Think of the surprise and gratitude he must have felt when Palmer invited him to a meal one evening. When he arrived he was confronted with Palmer; Jeremiah Smith, the local solicitor; Samuel Cheshire, the postmaster; William Saunders, the horse trainer; and possibly one other, a young gentleman, John Parsons Cook. In such distinguished company he must have felt highly honoured.

During the meal the conversation turned to life insurance and in particular one for George. To make it appear a great deal for him Palmer promised him that he would get £2,000 when the policy of £10,000 was paid out. George was amazed, probably seeing it as a way to get his farm back. There was only one snag which poor George had not realised – you had to be dead for the policy to pay out! Fully duped George agreed and Palmer began to search for a company.

The Midland Insurance Company finally agreed to sell a policy, but before they did, and unbeknown to Palmer, they sent two agents to Rugeley to interview the candidate. Palmer and friends had told the company that George Bates was a wealthy farmer, free of debt and with a sizeable income. However, when Mr. Field and Mr. Simpson, the two agents, arrived in Rugeley they met George dressed in rags and digging turnips in a field. He was obviously no country gentleman and so the company turned down the proposal. I like to think of George Bates as the one who got away. Had he been accepted he would surely have followed Annie and Walter to the grave.

Having been unsuccessful in his last two efforts to get money from insurance frauds Palmer must have by then been quite desperate, but it was not long before opportunity presented him with yet another possible victim. John Parsons Cook, a young wealthy gentleman from Lutterworth in Leicestershire, had become friends with Palmer sometime in 1853. They both were interested in racing and both had horses stabled with William Saunders at Hazel Slade. The two were regularly seen at local races together including those at Etching Hill, Rugeley, but whilst Palmer's horses were beginning to win less and less Cook's fortunes were on the up. In particular he had one very good horse, Polestar, which he had entered for the Shrewsbury Cup valued at over £2,000 to the winner.

November, 1855 saw both men at Shrewsbury Races along with Jeremiah Smith, Mr. Cheshire and William Saunders. Palmer's horses were not doing well again, but Polestar won the Shrewsbury Cup netting his owner around £3,000 in prize money and bets. As a celebration the company retired to the Raven Hotel in Shrewsbury where they had a meal together. Unfortunately for Cook, during the meal he drank a glass of brandy which made his throat burn and so he had to retire to bed. The landlady was to give evidence later that she had seen Palmer "putting something into Mr. Cook's brandy". The following day, despite still feeling unwell, Cook decided to stay at the races with Palmer (Smith and Cheshire having left) and at the close of the meeting Cook decided to return with Palmer to Rugeley where he booked in at the Talbot Arms which was straight across the road from Palmer's home. In fact the room that he had looked out at Palmer's residence.

13. The Shrew, once the Talbot Arms.

That same evening the two had a meal together, but once again Cook had to retire to bed feeling unwell. The following day, November 18th, Palmer sent over some broth for his friend to have, but Cook was unable to stomach it. Elizabeth Mills, the chambermaid, not wanting to see perfectly good food go to waste, drank it herself, but was sick soon after. On November 19th Palmer disappeared from Rugeley. He had taken Cook's betting book, caught the train down to London and had proceeded to collect Cook's betting winnings. Meanwhile back in Rugeley Cook was being cared for by Dr. Jones who actually stayed with his patient in his room all the time.

On his return to Rugeley Palmer continued to visit Cook and prescribe pills which Jones administered, but Cook was not recovering at all. At midnight on November 21st Jones sent for Palmer fearful that Cook was dying. Strangely Palmer arrived within minutes and fully dressed. Had he been waiting for the inevitable? Once in the room he administered two ammonia pills which he made up whilst in the room. (Apparently ammonia pills evaporate quickly and so have to be made up on the spot.) During that night Cook died a most painful and violent death despite the actions of Dr. Jones.

No one suspected foul play at the time as Cook had been ill for a few days, not even Dr. Jones, but Palmer had not counted on Mr. William Stevens, Cook's guardian. He had arrived from Leicestershire and was suspicious from the start. He quickly returned to Lutterworth to try to trace his ward's will, but on not finding it raced back to Rugeley. Once there he was amazed to find that Palmer had already ordered Cook's coffin and had started to arrange the funeral. His suspicions were greatly enhanced when Palmer tried to tell him that Cook had outstanding bills of some £4,000 though Palmer could not offer any proof (nor could he produce Cook's

betting book). It was at that point that Stevens insisted on an inquest despite Palmer's protests.

The inquest was duly arranged and a post mortem was ordered. Dr. Harland from Stafford was to take charge of the post mortem, but instead of performing it himself he got a student, Charles Devonshire, and Charles Newton, assistant to Mr. Salt the Rugeley chemist, to do it. Neither had ever done a post mortem in their lives! What followed was a complete farce. It took place in the public room of the Talbot Inn (not to be confused with the Talbot Arms

14. Grave of John Parsons Cook at St. Augustine's.

where Cook died) and quite a crowd gathered to watch. The body was hacked about and stomach samples taken from the room and then returned with absolutely no knowledge of what had happened to them whilst they were out of the room. Stevens was furious and demanded a second post mortem. It was granted but not at Rugeley. The stomach contents and other bits were sent to London to be examined by Dr. Taylor of St. Guy's Hospital, considered to be the pre-eminent pathologist of the day.

Palmer was getting worried and attempted to bribe the coroner with various gifts, urging him to give a verdict of death by natural causes. Fortunately the coroner would have none of it. Palmer also discovered that Dr. Taylor was sending his results by post and so he persuaded his friend, Mr. Cheshire, the postmaster, to let him see the letter before it went to the coroner; an offence resulting in gaol if caught. Palmer must have been elated when he read the results – NO poison found, but he was not to be happy for long. Dr. Taylor arrived to give evidence at the inquest on December 15th. There Taylor insisted that, despite no poison having been detected, Cook had died from strychnine poisoning. Dr. Jones' description of Cook's last hours and horrific death had convinced him of that. (Apparently strychnine sends the body's nervous system into reverse and eventually the spine snaps, killing the sufferer.)

15. Possible site of the old Post Office in Albion Street.

The jury took little time to conclude that Palmer had murdered Cook and officers were sent to arrest him. He was at home, ill in bed and already under house arrest for forgery. Thomas Woolllaston, a Police Officer at the time, kept a diary of his duties and it was subsequently turned into a book entitled *Police Experiences,* by Martin Woollaston. In it Thomas explains: - *"Palmer had placed himself in the hands of a friend from whom he had loans. It was discovered that this money lender had a bill for £1,000, purporting to have been accepted by his mother."* When he tried to get the money back she declared that *"she had not accepted it (signed the bill of debt with a promise to repay it if her son defaulted) and that she had no knowledge of its existence until applied to for payment."* When the case came to trial and while Palmer was awaiting the trial for murder it was found that the signature was a forgery, *"the name of his mother not being her signature, but written (at his instigation) by his wife, since deceased."* As for Palmer's love for his wife Thomas writes: - *"The prisoner, Palmer, after his wife's death, did not scruple to brand her memory with the stigma of conniving at and being instrumental in the crime of forgery."*

On his arrest Palmer was taken to Stafford Gaol on December 16th to await trial. Some days later, because rumours had started to circulate about the deaths of Annie and Walter, the Secretary of State was asked to order the exhumation of their bodies. He agreed and their post mortems took place at the Talbot Inn. Walter's body had deteriorated so much that nothing could be done, but Annie's body was still good enough to examine. It was discovered that she too had been poisoned, but that time by antimony. The inquest, therefore, brought in a verdict of murder by Palmer.

Incidentally the Talbot Inn, the place for many inquests and post mortems and also auctions in Rugeley, closed not many years later. Dave Lewis in his book The Rugeley Poisoner says, "The smell from the opening of Walter's coffin persisted for months and some say even years. They removed the wallpaper and sanded the floorboards in an attempt to rid them of the lingering smell. The publican complained bitterly that it ruined his trade and eventually the inn closed down."

After the inquests such was the hatred for Palmer that his friends and legal advisors, in the interests of securing a fair trial, questioned whether the trial should take place in the area and requested it be transferred to London. A special Act of Parliament had to be passed and then he was moved to London where the trial would eventually take place at the Central Criminal Court. That law gained the nickname of Palmer's Law in the Press.

Before the trial took place Palmer's assets were stripped to pay for the lawyers for his defence. All his stable of horses was sold off at an auction held at Tattersalls and raised over £3,000. In an article written covering the sale the reporter wrote, "A large majority of the miscellaneous assemblage, however, consisted of persons whose only motive was evidently to satisfy a feeling of curiosity which the circumstances with the sale had excited."

And that sense of morbid excitement would continue throughout his eventual trial with the Press making the most of the situation. In fact there was no law at the time which stopped reporters from interviewing people directly involved in the case. *The London Illustrated News,* one of the best sources of information on Palmer's trial, scoured the capital looking for witnesses and sketched everyone who appeared at the trail. Reporters were dispatched to Rugeley to sketch any place remotely connected with the case; incidentally leaving local historians with an excellent picture of Rugeley in the 1850's. As they do today, if given the chance, the reporters were quick describe the morbid and to apportion guilt. With such a Press free-for-all it was no wonder that Palmer would never get his fair hearing.

The trial began on May 14th, 1856 and was to last twelve days. Despite being implicated in the murders of Annie and Walter the case only concerned the death of John Parsons Cook. Once again it centred on the lack of poison discovered in Cook's body with each set of lawyers producing experts who gave conflicting theories. The Defence argued that the lack of poison found in the corpse meant there was no poisoning, while the Prosecution argued that it had disappeared due to the botched post mortem. The Prosecution produced key witnesses like Elizabeth Mills, the chambermaid, who told her story of the broth, and Charles Newton, the assistant chemist, who related how Palmer had bought strychnine on the evening of December 19th. Strangely other possible witnesses were not called. The Defence, even more strangely, neglected to produce the same people.

Palmer was doomed and was not helped by a lack lustre Defence team. Also the Prosecution had their trump card in Sir Alexander Cockburn, the leading barrister of the day. It was to be his last trial before being elevated to a judge and he was determined not to lose. His summation took over six hours and such was his persuasive speech that the jury took only an hour to return a verdict of WILFUL MURDER. Lord Chief Justice Campbell described Palmer's inevitable fate as follows:- *"Whether it is the first and only offence of this sort which you have committed, it is certainly known only to God and to your own conscience. It is seldom that such a familiarity with the means of death should be shown without long experience; but for this offence of which you have been found guilty your life is forfeited."* Obviously the judge was inferring that he knew of the other charges of murder involving Annie and Walter, but was there some niggling doubt in his mind that the Prosecution had been somewhat lucky with the verdict?

What then possibly made the judge uncomfortable? It is difficult to think that our modern justice system would allow a case of poisoning to go to court if no poison had been discovered, forensic experts would have a field day. As to the buying of the poison Charles Newton said that Palmer purchased it before nine o'clock on November 19th. That was the day that Palmer had been in London and, according to one witness for the Defence, Jeremiah Smith, Palmer had not got back until ten o'clock that evening. Unfortunately for the Defence, Jeremiah's character was ripped apart by the Prosecution when they revealed that Jeremiah was having an affair with Mrs. Palmer, William's elderly mother, and had been for over two years.

But what of the Station Master at Stafford? Surely he would have remembered a well-dressed gentleman getting off the train from London that late at night among only a few passengers? Strangely he was never called to give evidence. What about the gig driver who took Palmer back to Rugeley from Stafford late that night? He had simply disappeared. It was discovered later that he had been found a position up in the Staffordshire Moorlands and had not heard of the case. He was illiterate and newspapers probably would not find their way to such a remote place.

It is also quite probable that the gig driver had been "bought off". Sergeant Bergman of the Staffordshire Police had found him the position, but so what? In Staffordshire Record Office there are a series of letters written between Palmer and a Jane Bergman and relating to abortion. The two had been having an affair since 1855 resulting in Jane's pregnancy. Now if Jane and the Sergeant were somehow related then it does not take long to make two and two add up. Finally what of the chambermaid? Elizabeth Mills' evidence was so obviously coached the jury should have been wary. She was also illiterate, but showed no signs of nervousness or stammering or confusion throughout, relating the events in terms which would have been impossible for one of such low educational standards.

Whatever we may think Palmer was sentenced to be hanged in Stafford Gaol. He arrived by train, transported from Newgate Prison, at 12 p.m. May 27th in the charge of two warders. Police Officer Woollaston takes up the story.

"I attended Stafford Station with several constables. On the prisoner's alighting from the train he recognised me and, taking my arm, asked to be allowed to walk with me; that he did the whole way to the County Gaol. In the confusion which ensued when passing up the streets, caused by the anxiety of the crowd to see the prisoner, many were upset and trampled upon, and the scene and improper epithets indulged in were indecent in the extreme. The prisoner was heavily ironed and walked with difficulty; his manacles were hidden from view by a large prison cloak."

Woollaston was also present at Palmer's execution on June 14th, 1856 when he was hanged outside the gaol in front of a huge crowd of over 30,000. He writes, *"I saw the prisoner executed and was also afterwards present when a cast of his head and face was taken."* So ended the career of Rugeley's most infamous resident.

But not quite; for years after others were to speak of their own near fatal brushes with the doctor, but should they be taken with the proverbial pinch of salt. Most certainly the story of Rugeley people wanting to change the town's name because of its notoriety should. It was rumoured that they sent a petition to Parliament asking to have the town's name changed, something almost unheard of in those days. Obviously Parliament disagreed, but came up with a solution to stop the petitions in their tracks. Rugeley could change its name, but only if it took the name of the Prime Minister – one Lord Palmerston. One suspects the newspapers may just have invented the story to keep their sales going longer.

*William Brookes Palmer, the only surviving child, left Rugeley and went to London where he worked as a solicitor. He died in May, 1926 at the age of 76. His death certificate reads:- "Syncope and asphyxia. Coal gas poisoning – misadventure." The gas tap had been left on.

*There were other casualties of this tragic story. Samuel Cheshire, the postmaster, did not escape justice. In March, 1856 he was convicted of opening Royal Mail at the Rugeley Post Office and given a twelve month prison sentence as well as losing his position. William Saunders, Palmer's horse trainer, suffered when he lost almost half of his stable of thoroughbreds and it took him years to recover.

MY MONEY OR YOUR LIFE
Cannock

Money, or more correctly the lack of it, has always been a strong motive for crime and the police spend a great deal of their time investigating burglary and robbery. However, there are other motives for crimes involving cash. What about the grievance someone may feel for money owing to them for a job done? The longer the debt goes unpaid the more aggrieved the person will begin to feel until rage begins to fester and when the two protagonists eventually meet disaster can easily happen. That was the case with two incidents recorded here, curiously enough involving the Crown Hotel in Cannock. Whatever the cause of the crime, the old adage that "money is the root of all evil" certainly runs true in the following incidents.

Tuesday, October 18th, 1836 was a pleasant day when at ten minutes to one Matthias Willington Stringer entered the Crown Hotel in Cannock and called for three pennyworth of gin (a cheap and common drink for the working classes in those days). A kitchen labourer at the inn he was probably readying himself for his day's work. Having got the drink he sat himself down by the fireplace to rest. A few minutes later James Hawkins, gamekeeper to Lord Lichfield, came in and Stringer spotted him. Without waiting for Hawkins to settle down, Stringer shouted across the room that Hawkins owed him money for "destroying some game eight years ago". Trying to calm the situation Hawkins sat down with Stringer and the two seemed to be having a quiet conversation. Suddenly the men erupted and began struggling with one another over a dog which Stringer had taken from Hawkins.

16. The Crown Hotel, Cannock c.1880.

33

Hawkins threatened Stringer with a stick and during the struggle he pulled out a pistol and shot him. Stringer immediately fell to the floor and died within seconds.

After the commotion died down Hawkins was taken to the local lock-up to await the inquest and subsequent trial. It must be said that he offered no resistance to his arrest, possibly confident that in the fight he had not been the aggressor and had merely defended himself, even though he did use a gun to kill Stringer. Would the inquest court see the incident in the same manner? They did not – and committed Hawkins to Stafford Gaol to await trial for murder.

That trial took place on Thursday, March 16th, 1837 in front of Judge Baron Holland. The Counsel for the Prosecution, Mr. Phillips, began by outlining the incident at the Crown Hotel on October 18th and then called the first witness. William Whitehouse of Cheslyn Hay told the court that he had been at the Crown that afternoon when the deceased entered, shortly followed by the prisoner. He told the court that as soon as Hawkins entered the inn Stringer shouted, *"Oh, Hawkins, you owe me some money! I wish you would pay it!"* Hawkins then replied, *"I owe you nothing that I know of and nothing I'll pay you."* Stringer then retaliated, *"Why, you owe me five shillings, but I'll take up with half a crown and half a crown I'll have!"* The prisoner then said, *"I do not know what I owe you anything for,"* upon which the deceased replied, *"It was for destroying some game eight years ago."* Hawkins then said, *"Why, it is so long since, I hope you'll not repeat any old grievances over."*

Stringer persisted saying that he would have his half crown and in an attempt to calm the situation down Hawkins said that he would not argue any longer and gave the deceased his jug to drink with him. Stringer took the jug and drank and

17. Police on duty opposite St. Luke's, Cannock.

Hawkins sat down. The deceased sat with him in a chair opposite but quite close to the prisoner as if in a threatening manner. Both men then seated Stringer said, *"I'll have the half crown or else you shall fight me,"* to which Hawkins replied, *"I'll not fight you. I did not come here to fight."* Once again the argument seemed to subside.

However, it began once again. Hawkins had a little dog with him and the deceased picked that dog up and placed it on his own lap. Annoyed Hawkins pulled the dog off and gave it a rap with a hazel stick which he had in his hand and told the dog to go under his seat. Stringer asked him what he had hit the dog for and immediately grabbed hold of the stick to take it from the prisoner. They struggled, each having hold of the stick with both hands and endeavouring to get possession of it. Hawkins told the deceased to let go of it and added, *"If you do not let go I'll drill a hole through you!"* Stringer refused and Hawkins let go of it with his right hand and drew a small pocket pistol from his left hand side jacket pocket and dropped his hand by his right thigh.

At that point the deceased rose slightly from his chair, let go of the stick and made a grab for the pistol which was still down by the prisoner's thigh. The prisoner pulled his hand back, both men raised their hands and the pistol fired. When it went off the deceased was standing, but the prisoner was still sitting. The pistol ball entered the left side of Stringer's temple and he dropped and never spoke or stirred afterwards. At that point the witness left the room and went into another returning about a quarter of an hour later.

Under cross-examination by Mr. Sergeant Ludlow acting for the Defence, Whitehouse said that before Stringer had come into the inn he had already been "leathering" a young man outside. He also said that he saw "no offensive conduct by the prisoner towards the deceased." As far as he knew the two men had agreed to "fight at the races" some days later. (Those races were to be held at Hednesford on Friday, November 6th. See *Hednesford's Horse Racing History* also by your author.) Obviously Counsel for the Defence was trying to sway the jury in favour of his own client.

The court then heard similar evidence from Thomas Beddow, Thomas Woodhall and Samuel Whitehouse all representing the deceased to have been the aggressor and that the prisoner repeatedly tried to calm the situation and avoid any quarrel. However, the next witness, Francis Saunders, a butty collier living in Cannock, was not so favourable to the prisoner.

Francis stated that he was also at the Crown Hotel on October 18th when the argument took place. He said that the first thing that he heard was the prisoner saying, *"Damn your blood, I have been the bringing up of you all in this part of the country and if you use me in this way I will drill a hole through you!"* (Hawkins was probably referring to supplying the men with illegal game.) Francis also stated that he did not see a stick at the time. The deceased then said something about some money which the prisoner owed him and they got up and were disputing about it.

The company at the inn interposed and endeavoured to persuade them to sit down and be quiet. They did sit down and in a few minutes the prisoner jumped up out of his chair, pulled out half a crown and offered to fight the deceased for five pounds. The deceased then pulled out a half crown and one of the coins fell to the floor.

The two men then sat down facing very much near to each other. The deceased picked up a dog and placed it on his lap. The prisoner then pulled it off his lap by the tail and placed it by the side of him. He then hit the dog with a stick. Both of the men then laid hold of the stick with both hands and there was some struggling between them to get hold of it. The prisoner then loosed the stick with his right hand, put it towards his left hand side pocket and drew out a pistol of which the witness took very particular notice.

¼d.	ONE FARTHING	10p
½d.	ONE HALFPENNY (ha'penny)	20p
¾d.	THREE FARTHINGS	30p
1d.	ONE PENNY	40p
1¼d.	A PENNY FARTHING	50p
2½d.	TWOPENCE HA'PENNY	£1.00
3d.	THREEPENCE	£1.20
6d.	SIXPENCE	£2.40
1 l- d.	ONE SHILLING	£4.80
1 l 0½d.	ONE AND A HA'PENNY	£5.00
2 l 1d.	TWO AND A PENNY	£10.00
10 l - d.	TEN SHILLINGS	£48.00
£1 l- l - d.	ONE POUND	£96.00

18. Table of Monetary Values around 1840.

Whilst it was beside the prisoner's thigh the witness saw him cock it with his thumb. The prisoner then told the deceased that if he did not give over he would drill a hole through him. The deceased then rose from his seat nearly upright and then stooped down to lay hold of the prisoner's right hand and the witness believed he caught hold of it a little above the wrist, but he did not grasp the arm. The prisoner immediately drew his hand from under the deceased's arm, turned around a little, and shot the deceased who instantly fell down and expired.

The next witness was the Reverend G.B. Latimer who stated that he was standing within the doorway of the Crown Hotel at Cannock on October 18th when he heard the report of a pistol from inside. He went immediately into the tap room and saw the prisoner sitting in the room. He had a pistol in his hand. The witness then said that he asked those present who shot the deceased and the prisoner replied, *"I am the man. I shot him and I know what I have done."* The prisoner then gave the witness the pistol and he handed it over to James Jeffreys. Jeffreys then told the court that he had handed the pistol over to Mr. William Cope.

William Cope was next to give evidence. He stated that he was a draper living in Cannock and had received the pistol from Mr. Jeffreys. At that point he produced the pistol in court and showed it to the judge and jury. It was a small pocket pistol with a percussion lock. (Readers may be amazed to see that the evidence was held by Mr. Cope, a draper. The 1830's was very early in the life of the police force and Cannock almost certainly did not have a regular constabulary at the time. Local constables were elected by the town council and frequently had other occupations.)

Mr. Cope then stated that he was present when the prisoner was in the lock-up and the prisoner had said to him, *"You have no need to search me for that is the only one I have got."* He had also asked the prisoner why he had shot Stringer to which the prisoner replied, *"If he had let me alone I should not have done it."* At the end of his evidence he also produced the hazel stick for the court to examine.

Thomas Trevor Holland, the Cannock surgeon, was the next to give his statement. He said that he was called to the Crown Hotel to view the deceased. He found him still lying on the floor of the inn and bleeding. He examined the head and found that some substance had passed through the temporal bone. He put his finger into the hole and felt the brain. On Thursday October 20th he opened the head and discovered a pistol ball which he estimated would produce instant death. The ball had passed through the brain and fractured the skull on the other side. While the body was in his care Thomas Stringer, the deceased's uncle, had identified it.

The Prosecution having concluded Mr. Sergeant Ludlow for the Defence rose to address the jury. Not doubting that his client had shot the deceased he laboured the points of law concerning murder, that being the deliberate taking of a life. He argued that the prisoner's actions were not murder. There were two other possibilities – either that the pistol went off accidentally or that the circumstances of the argument not brought about by his client were such as to reduce the act to the crime of manslaughter. He finally closed his address after one hour and twenty minutes by a powerful appeal to the feelings of the jury and implored them to ponder well before they gave their verdict.

Having duly considered the evidence the jury gave their verdict after an hour – GUILTY of MURDER, but recommended the prisoner to mercy. The judge stated that unfortunately he owed his judgement of sentence to the public and had no other option but to pass a sentence of death. Hawkins, on hearing the sentence, collapsed in the dock and had to be carried away to await his fate. There was, however, a final twist to the story – rather than execution Hawkins was TRANSPORTED to the colonies, probably Australia.

The next case sees another two men fighting over owed money and again the action happened at the Crown Hotel, Cannock. On Monday, January 28th, 1901 Edward Walker, aged 30, a horse breaker/trainer from Cooper's Coppice, Cannock Wood, arrived at the Crown Hotel in Cannock in the early afternoon and wanted to stable his two horses there. William Henry Broom, aged 32, the ostler at the inn, demanded that Walker pay him one shilling there and then. An argument broke out about the price (usually six pence) and without warning Broom struck out at Walker. In the ensuing scuffle Broom was knocked on to the footpath with Walker on top of him. After a further few minutes the fight ended and Broom went home which was in Mill Street. Unfortunately he died the following morning at around 7.30 a.m. and Walker was arrested.

At a specially convened police court on Wednesday before the magistrate, Mr. F.D. Bumsted, the only witness to give evidence was Inspector Burgess who stated that he had arrested Walker at 10.30 p.m. the day before at Cooper's Coppice, near Hazel Slade and cautioned him. Walker had asked when Broom had died and on being told said, *"He came messing round me and wanted a shilling from me for stabling two horses. He (Broom) struck at me and I gave him one and knocked him down. He got up and pulled off his jacket and wanted to fight me up the yard. I am very sorry. It is a bad job for all parties."* At that stage in the proceedings Walker was remanded in custody until the following Monday. His father-in-law was the surety and the bail required was £10 with a surety of a further £10.

The inquest into Broom's death took place at the Crown Hotel on Thursday afternoon before Mr. S.W. Morgan, the coroner, and a jury of whom Mr. Cross was the foreman. Mr. S.E. Loxton, the solicitor, appeared for Walker.

19. The Crown Hotel, Cannock c.1920.

The first witness was Ellen Broom, wife of William Broom, a labourer of Mill Street. She gave evidence of identification of her son's body and added that the deceased lived with her in Mill Street. On January 28th he came home at about 6.15 p.m. and said to his father, *"Look at my face, dad, where that man kicked me. Do you think my eye will go black?"* His father said that he thought that it would not. He refused anything to eat and asked his mother to place a pillow on the sofa for him to lie down. He never spoke to her again. At about 11.00 p.m. the witness went to bed, leaving her son asleep on the sofa. At 6.00 a.m. the next morning she got up and went to look at her son who was still apparently asleep on the sofa.

In attempt to rouse him she called out *"Will! Will!"* and as he did not answer she said, *"Son, speak to your mother!"* He moved a little and threw up some blood from his mouth and nose. She kept a careful watch over him and at 7.30 a.m. when she saw no signs of life she sent for Dr. Butter at about 8.00 a.m. Unfortunately the doctor was out and when he did arrive her son was pronounced dead.

Under questioning from Mr. Loxton Mrs. Broom had to admit that her son had arrived home that afternoon "not sober, but he appeared stunned". He had come home the worse for beer on other occasions. As to his injuries she said that up to 11.00 p.m. she saw nothing to make her think that his condition was serious enough to call for a doctor. He had not complained of any pain in his head and as far as she knew he had made his own way home. Finally she said that the sofa on which her son lay was in the same room where she and her husband slept.

William Drake, a miner from Stafford Road, Cannock, was next to give evidence. He stated that on Monday, January 28th he was outside the Crown Hotel when Walker came up to him and asked if he would hold his horse. As he was holding the horse Broom came out of the stable yard and caught hold of the bridle and demanded his money. Just at that moment Walker came up to them and Broom said something to him. A scuffle took place and both men fell to the ground. The witness could not tell who was on top as the men were rolling around. When they got up Broom's mouth was bleeding, though not very much. The next time he saw Broom he had his jacket off and was sparring at Walker.

Drake then continued. He said that he could not see much more of the fight as the crowd that had gathered obstructed his view. The next thing he saw was Walker and the young man who was with him riding away on the horses. After that he noticed Broom standing in Market Place and he did not seem much hurt. As far as he was concerned Walker only defended himself and Broom was the aggressor. He never saw Walker kick or use any unfair means to injure Broom and Walker did not take off his own jacket during the scuffle. When asked by Dr. Butter about the "rolling around on the ground" Drake said that both men's heads were towards the kerbstones as they rolled.

Another witness to the fight was Robert Stephens, a fish hawker from Cannock Road, Chadsmoor. He stated that on the Monday afternoon at around 3.30 p.m. he was at the blacksmith's shop opposite the Crown Hotel. He went across Market Square and saw Broom with his jacket off. He heard Broom shout, *"Let him come outside!"* and Walker came out of the vaults. Broom went up to Walker and struck at him. They then wrestled and both fell to the ground rolling about. Walker got on top and while he had his one knee in Broom's stomach he held Broom's hands in one hand and hit the deceased in the face twice with the other. Just then a butcher named Guy of Green Heath, Hednesford caught hold of Walker and got him on to his horse. While on his horse Walker said, *"If I get off again I'll strangle you!"*

Questioned by Mr. Loxton Stephens said that when Broom struck at Walker the latter seized Broom by the throat, but if he had not done so Broom would have stuck him again. Leaving the witness the coroner and jury then left the hotel and went outside to examine the spot where the fight took place. On their return Stephens continued his evidence. He said that the deceased was lying head downwards towards the hotel with the right side of his head nearest the wall. The witness did not see Broom's head strike the stone which projects from the wall nor did he see Walker kick Broom. He told the inquest that he actually stayed with the deceased until 5.00 p.m. and had a drink with him in the Crown. At that point the coroner closed the inquest until Inspector Burgess could interview further witnesses (some fifteen or sixteen persons had witnessed the fight) and Br. Butter could give evidence as to the post mortem results.

20. Police on duty in Market Place, Cannock.

On resuming the inquest on Tuesday, February 5th the first new witness was John Crabtree, a miner living in Walsall Road, Cannock. He stated that he saw the deceased try to take the horse from William Drake and then saw Walker come out of the hotel and try to take the reins back off Broom. Both men were talking about the stable money and they closed with each other and both men fell to the ground. Walker was on top and hit Broom in the mouth. They both got up and Walker went back into the vaults. The deceased then pulled off his jacket and said he would wait until Walker came out again. As Walker was going to get back on his horse Broom went at him and again the men closed and fell down together, Walker being on top with his knee on Broom. Walker then took hold of Broom's hands and threatened to strike him, but the witness did not see Walker strike the deceased. After that Walker got up, mounted his horse and rode away.

Questioned by Mr. Loxton Crabtree said the blow in the mouth was the only one he witnessed and he did not see Walker kick the deceased. When questioned by Mr. Cross, the foreman of the jury, the witness said that he did not think a previous witness, Drake, was in a good position to see everything that took place. When Dr. Butter questioned him Crabtree stated that he saw Broom's head strike the ground as the men fell, but he never saw his head strike the wall.

Elizabeth Waldron, wife of Thomas Waldron, of Huntington Terrace, Chadsmoor stated that at about 4.00 p.m. she was standing in Market Place when she saw Broom trying to take a horse from a man outside the Crown Hotel. She then saw Walker come out of the hotel and shout, *"Loose that ---- horse: it's mine!"* Broom refused and said, *"I want my stabling,"* and Walker replied, *"I have paid it in the house."* Broom replied, *"You will have to pay me."* (She had heard him ask for sixpence.) Then the men had a bit of a struggle and Broom fell on the ground with Walker stooping over him. She saw Walker hit Broom in the mouth while he was on the ground. Walker then pulled the deceased up by his neckerchief and left him sitting on the pavement. When Broom fell he dropped on his head.

Questioned by Mr. Cross Elizabeth said that she was sure that Broom's head caught the ground, striking it heavily. When Inspector Burgess questioned her she said that Walker *"caught hold of Broom by the scarf round his neck and hurled him on the floor"*. Readers may notice how the female perception of a fight is more vicious than a male's might be, probably because women see fighting as a savage remnant of human development.

Ernest Roberts, son of the landlady of the Crown Hotel, stated that he first saw the deceased at 3.15 p.m. on the fatal day in the kitchen of the hotel and at the time he was the worse for drink. Broom was temporarily employed as an ostler at the hotel. At that time Walker was already in the vaults (one of the rooms in the hotel usually selling spirits as well as ale and nothing to do with cellars). The deceased had been away from the hotel for several hours and the witness had told him that it would be better if he went home and so Broom went out. The next thing he heard was Broom asking Walker for sixpence, the stable money. Broom came to the counter and the witness told him to go home and that he would see to the stable money. The witness then saw someone come in and speak to Walker who went outside.

From the smoke room window Robert stated that he saw Broom trying to take the reins of the horse out of Drake's hands. Walker then went up and tried to take the reins away from Broom. He did not see any blows struck as he was called away. Walker came back in a few minutes afterwards and asked how much the stabling was. Witness replied, *"Never mind that, it will do some other time."* Walker then went outside again and the witness said that he returned to the smoke room window.

He saw that Broom had his jacket off, but he did not see any blows struck. Shortly after that he heard someone say, *"Ernest, they have gone to fight in the yard."* He went out and saw Walker on top of the deceased and clutching his throat. The witness then said, *"What are you doing here? Get off him and clear out."* At that the deceased got up and the witness noticed he was bleeding badly at the mouth. After washing himself Broom came into the hotel and the witness gave him his wages and dismissed him.

When questioned by Mr. Loxton Ernest Roberts said that Walker was present when he had told the deceased to *"never mind the stabling money"*. On answering questions by Inspector Burgess Roberts said that Broom had been employed by the hotel for about two months and it was the deceased's job to collect the stabling money which he paid to either himself or Mrs. Roberts every evening. However, it was against the rules to take money inside the hotel. There had been some haggling about the money in the vaults and that was why he had told Walker to never mind it. He added that if Broom had allowed anyone to take their horse away without paying Broom would have been held responsible.

The final person to give evidence at the inquest was Dr. Butter. At the post mortem he had found a lot of bruises over the head and face extending down the neck on each side. There was also an abrasion on the brow over the right eye and another, the size of a threepenny piece, over the bridge of the nose. The face was very much discoloured, the lips being purple and swollen. There was a bruise on the left arm and one on the right elbow. Several bruises were scattered over the left forearm and wrist and a large swelling over the left temple. Internally, underneath the swelling, there was a large effusion of blood. On opening the brain he had found a large clot of blood lying on and compressing the left half of the brain and an artery had been torn. The clot of blood was the cause of death.

Further examination of Broom's corpse showed signs of damage to the lungs, liver, kidneys and heart, probably brought on by his excessive drinking. However, it was the clot which had caused death and which was caused by violence. He thought, however, that the injury must have been caused by a more severe blow than a fist could give. It might have been caused by a fall. The man being a confirmed alcohol drinker rendered his blood vessels more liable to give way. Finally Dr. Butter agreed that the injury might have been caused by a kick or a fall.

After reviewing the evidence the coroner instructed the jury that if they agreed that the clot of blood had been caused as a result of violence by Walker or caused by the fall while in the act of fighting then they should bring in a verdict of manslaughter. After about twenty minutes private discussion they returned the verdict of manslaughter. Walker would go to trial at the next Stafford Assizes.

The trial took place at Stafford Assizes on Friday, March 15th 1901 with Mr. Graham for the Prosecution and Mr. Kettle for the Defence. Mr. Graham outlined the case and then all the witnesses from the inquest were heard. William Sansom, the manager of a boot shop in Market Place, Cannock added further evidence. He stated that he saw the deceased strike the prisoner on the cheek. A struggle followed during which the prisoner struck the deceased, but it was not a violent blow. Bernard Sharp, who had ridden to Cannock with Walker, stated that he saw the deceased strike the prisoner on the neck when asked to let go the reins. The prisoner hit Broom in the mouth and they both fell down, the deceased striking left and right at Walker, who did not retaliate, but simply seized him and pushed him back. Evidence for the Defence was also given by William Guy, a butcher from Hednesford; John Sellman, a cabman from Cannock; and Herbert Marshall, a butcher from Chadsmoor.

Finally, Walker himself entered the witness box. He testified that he offered the deceased sixpence for the stabling and Broom replied, *"I will have a bob (shilling) or I'll knock it out of you."* The deceased refused to let go of the reins and struck the witness twice, on the cheek and on the chest. Seeing that Broom was coming at him to continue the fight he hit him in the mouth and that was the only blow that he struck. The deceased then grabbed hold of him and they both fell down. Under questioning Walker denied clutching Broom by the throat or striking him again. He also said that on the day he was sober whereas the deceased was "fresh".

In his submission to the jury Mr. Kettle argued that his client had used no more violence than anyone else would have done when attacked by a *"half drunken fellow like Broom who undoubtedly began the affray and was the aggressor"*.

The jury subsequently retired and after only fifteen minutes deliberation returned a verdict of ACQUITTAL. Walker went from the court a free man.

Historical note:- The Crown Hotel had long dominated Market Place in Cannock and had been a successful coaching inn for many years. Regular services ran between London, Manchester and Liverpool until the advent of the railways saw its gradual demise in the late nineteenth century. It was finally demolished in 1961 to make way for shops.

THE EVILS OF DRINK
Hednesford, Cannock and Chasetown

There are four types of drunk. Firstly, and the least harmless, are the ones who just want to go to sleep. As far as they are concerned the party's over and bed beckons. Secondly, there are those who become stupid and act daft, but they can put their lives and the lives of others around them in danger. All reason goes out of the window and they will do things that, when sober, they would never dream of doing. Thirdly, there are those who become morbid and depressed and want to share their worries with the world or at least with those unlucky enough to be with them. Lastly, there are those who want to fight everybody and the slightest provocation will get them squaring up to even their best friends. The following cases fall into one or other of the above categories.

On the evening of Saturday, August 3rd, 1929 a group of men left the Cross Keys Inn, Hednesford at about ten o'clock and headed up Hill Street towards Wood Lane. They were closely followed by another group of men going in the same direction. The first group of men consisted of Jim Roden, Chas Cotterell and his brother, Harry, Walter Westwood and William Ramsdale. The second four men were Gittings, Winfindale, Fownes and Meacham.

21. The Cross Keys and Hill Street, Hednesford c.1910.

At some point Jim Roden began an argument with Fownes from the second group, but after some persuasion that argument died down and Roden caught up with his party. However, he did not like being admonished by Chas Cotterell and must have gone to strike him. Unfortunately the scuffle which followed ended up with Roden falling to the ground where he hit his head. Cotterell walked away and not long after Roden got up and walked home. Everything seemed to have ended quite satisfactorily. When Roden arrived home he went to bed, but died sometime during the night. Because of the unusual circumstances of the death the police were called and Chas Cotterell was arrested on a charge of manslaughter.

After a preliminary hearing he was remanded to await trial before the magistrates at Cannock. On Tuesday August 13th Chas Cotterell, aged 27 of George Street, a colliery lamp cleaner, was brought before Cannock Police Court to answer the charge of manslaughter against Jim Roden, aged 20, also of George Street and a locomotive colliery fireman. The magistrates would determine whether Cotterell should face trial at the Assizes. Mr. McGregor Clarkson had been employed to defend him.

The first witness was Dr. Holton who repeated his evidence given at the inquest. He stated that the deceased had died from a fracture to the skull, which was only two thirds the thickness of a normal man. There were no external marks of violence. In reply to questions from Mr. Clarkson, Dr. Holton said that Roden was a fairly well-built man and apparently strong and healthy. He could not say what part of the head Roden had fallen on, but it was most likely the side. It was possible that the injury could have been caused by him falling on the bedroom floor, but he would have to have been standing up and not just have fallen out of bed as the distance from the bed to the floor was not great enough to cause such an injury.

In reply to a question from Mr. Orton, the deputy magistrates' clerk, Dr. Holton said that if a blow had been struck by some instrument or a weapon there would have been a bruise and none was found.

William Edward Ramsdale of 45 George Street said that he went to the Cross Keys Inn at 8.30 p.m. on the Saturday evening and left at 10.00 p.m. with the two Cotterells, Roden and Westwood. As they walked up Hill Street Roden and Chas Cotterell gradually dropped behind. As they reached Wood Lane he heard Roden and Cotterell talking, but could not hear exactly what they were saying as they were talking quietly. He then heard a scuffling of feet, looked round and saw Roden on the floor. He went over to him and saw that he was "knocked out".

He then turned to Cotterell and said, *"What have you done that for, Charlie?"* to which he replied, *"I don't know, I am sure."* One of the other men present said, *"You ought to be ashamed of yourself, Charlie"*, but Cotterell never replied. He just walked away. Roden, who still had his coat on, was eventually brought round and walked with them up the lane. Roden then left them and went home. The witness then said that he saw Cotterell several times after the incident and he said he was sorry it had happened. He once said, *"I would not have done it for all the world."*

When questioned by Mr. Clarkson William Ramsdale said that there was another group of men who came out of the Cross Keys at the same time. They included Gittings, Winfindale, Fownes and Meacham. Roden and Fownes started an argument and they wanted to fight, Fownes being the more eager. Cotterell and Roden were pals and the witness remembered Cotterell saying to Roden, *"Come on up the road. Let's have no bother."* They all started up the road, but they stopped again as Roden and Fownes were still arguing. He heard Meacham offer to fight Fownes. Eventually they all worked Meacham into a corner and persuaded him to be sensible. Fownes, Meacham, Winfindale and Gittings then went away.

Under further questioning he said that he saw Roden only have one pint of beer, but he was in the pub before the witness arrived. All of them had had some drink, more or less, the witness having two or three half pints. He had to agree that the *"absurd disputes and various challenges"* would never have happened if they had been sober. Those who argued were the ones who had had most beer.

The next witness was Walter Westwood of Platt Street, Hightown who said that he was with the group walking up Hill Street and as they got into Wood Lane he heard someone fall and went back to the man on the ground. Roden was lying on his back and the witness could see that he still had his hands in his trouser pockets. He was unconscious. He remembered that Cotterell had his coat off, but Roden still had his on.

22. The Cross Keys and Hill Street, Hednesford c.1920.

When questioned by Mr. Clarkson he said that after the two parties of men had separated their party had gone about a hundred yards when the scuffle occurred. As to Roden's hands he said that he could not be certain if the deceased had both hands in his trouser pockets, but he knew for certain that the left hand was in the trouser pocket because he took it out. Finally he said that they had all been drinking.

William Edward Gittings of Violet House, Hednesford said that when they reached the corner of George Street after the scuffle the accused had his jacket off and wanted to fight. He could not remember Cotterell's exact words, but they were something like, *"I have left one for dead down the road"* or *"I have left him for dead down the road."*

Under questioning Gittings said that nobody replied to Cotterell's challenge although previously Meacham from his group had responded to challenges, but no fight took place. Asked about their drinking he said that Roden looked and sounded sober. He too was *"quite sober",* but could not speak for the others although he thought they were *"pretty well sober".*

James Fownes of Lozells, Birmingham stated that he had come out of the Cross Keys at ten o'clock on that Saturday and Roden came up and spoke to him. There was a discussion about one of the witness's relatives and Roden made a remark which the witness resented. (Fownes did not relate that remark to the court as it was too personal and the court did not insist.) After the remark there looked like there could be trouble, but they were pulled away from each other. However, a little further up Hill Street the trouble started again. They eventually reached the corner of George Street and after the scuffle with Roden Cotterell came up to the witness and the others and said, *"I have left one for dead and I will fight any one of you."* At that point the accused had his coat and waistcoat off. The witness picked them up and tried to persuade Cotterell to put them on. He, however, said he would hit the witness if he did not move.

When questioned Fownes said that he would not fight Cotterell because he knew that the accused had a surgical boot and limped. He realised that Cotterell was *"very excited",* but would not say that he was drunk, neither would he say that he was perfectly sober. He would, however, say that they were all sober. (Conflicting statement which suggests the men's state of mind on the fatal night?) Fownes admitted quarrelling with Roden and remembered the latter saying, *"I don't care for you or anybody else."* He realised the deceased was "a bit touchy" and so said that he did not want any bother with him. He also remembered that Meacham wanted to fight him (the witness) because he said that he, the witness, would not listen to reason about the relative. The witness then told Meacham that if he wanted to fight he should wait until morning when he would better understand what Roden had said about the relative.

Once finished with the "evidence" from those involved the court heard from Police Constable Martin who stated that he had gone to interview the accused on August 5th at his home. Cotterell had simply said at that time, *"I wish to reserve my defence."* The next day he arrested him and the accused repeated the remark.

Eliza Roden stated that James Roden was her nephew and he had lived with her in George Street for some years as he had no parents. He had left the house at 7.00 p.m. on August 3rd and returned at 11.00 p.m. He had complained about Cotterell and all his clothes had mud on them. At first he lay on the sofa, but then went to bed. The witness followed him and covered him up. The following morning she went upstairs at ten o'clock and found him, as she thought, fast asleep. She went up again later and, realising that something was wrong, she sent for the doctor.

In reply to Mr. Clarkson she said that her nephew did not fall out of bed as she would have heard him if he had. She remembered calling at Cotterell's house, but she did not tell him that her nephew had fallen out of bed. When Mr. Clarkson told her that such a statement was attributed to her she said to the court, *"It is a lie, a deliberate lie."* Also she insisted that she had never said to anyone that she had gone into her nephew's room because she could not hear him breathing or that she had found him with his face down in the bedclothes.

Chas Cotterell, who pleaded not guilty, was then allowed to give his side of the story. He told the court that he and Roden were walking behind the others because he could not walk very fast and so Roden, his pal, walked with him. As they walked along he told the deceased to have no bother as he knew what Meacham was like. He had heard that Meacham had been fighting the previous Saturday with a man in Hazel Slade who was old enough to be his father. At that point Roden called him a liar, at the same time using a *"filthy adjective"*. Cotterell said that he resented that and so took off his overcoat and jacket and placed them on the bank.

Roden stood behind him, placed his hand on his shoulder and swung him round. Thinking Roden was going to hit him he "closed" with him and hit him for calling him a liar. The deceased seemed to stumble and then fell backwards. He insisted that he never said that he had left one for dead down the road. What he actually said was that he had left his pal lying in the road as if he were dead. About ten minutes after the scuffle he saw Roden walking home and he seemed perfectly alright.

Under further questioning he admitted that Roden never struck him. Roden was under the influence because when he walked he did so *"with a roll"*.

All evidence having been heard Mr. Clarkson addressed the magistrates. He said that it was doubtful whether any of the actual witnesses of the bother could remember what exactly took place. In view of their "condition" he suggested "their observation was somewhat clouded and their recollection dimmed". At least three of them, apart from the accused, had been drinking and when men got into that state little things seemed to irritate them. However, there was no evidence amongst all of the witnesses to a blow having been struck. There was nothing to suggest any instrument or weapon and the injury was consistent with a fall. It was even consistent with a fall in one's sleep. The men were not in a very good condition and it was not a difficult thing to suggest that they might have experienced many an accidental fall on their way home that night.

He continued saying that Cotterell and Roden were good pals and no one had suggested any reason for a dispute or that there had ever been any bad blood between them. The accused had actually succeeded in getting Roden away from a previous bother that night. If they assumed a blow was indeed struck then there was no question of a surprise attack because Cotterell took off some of his clothes and placed them on a bank. A man in a fuddled condition as he was would take some time to do that.

He told the magistrates that the fracture was the cause of death, but a jury would have to be satisfied that a blow caused it and Cotterell was the man who struck it. They had to remember that after the incident Roden walked up the road unaided.

Finally he stated that the evidence of some of the witnesses was unreliable, not because they were dishonest, but because their sobriety on the night was very doubtful. He, therefore, submitted that no jury would convict his client on a charge of manslaughter.

Unfortunately for Mr. Clarkson and Chas Cotterell the magistrates did not agree and he was committed to the next Assizes for the manslaughter of James Roden. His case came before Mr. Justice Acton on Monday, November 18th 1929 and once more Mr. Clarkson defended him. The only new evidence which appeared came from Dr. Holton when the judge asked him, *"Do you think it was possible or likely that after receiving that injury he could walk home some considerable number of yards, go into the house and sit up for twenty minutes or so and then go to bed without assistance?"* Dr. Holton replied, *"Yes, I think it is likely. The cause of death was haemorrhage which might have been going on all the time."*

Despite that new statement Mr. Clarkson reiterated that there was no actual evidence from any of the witnesses of any blow having been struck. Roden might merely have fallen down himself as he was under the influence and hit his head on the ground. Cotterell, in his own inebriated state, might have thought that he hit him, but in fact his attempt never made contact. The jury agreed and returned a verdict of NOT GUILTY and Cotterell walked free.

It is a well known scientific fact that alcohol affects the female brain far quicker than the male and the female capacity is far lower. Now if some men have a tendency to become violent when inebriated it must surely follow that some women may also lean towards that pattern. I can remember being warned years ago that "there is nothing worse than a drunken woman". Perhaps the next episode highlights that theory.

In November 1889 Cannock's polite society was rocked and astounded by rumours of a dreadful stabbing perpetrated by a woman and many people were eager to know all about the affair. The preliminary case was heard on Monday, November 4th at Cannock Petty Sessions before Messrs. Gilpin, Vernon and Bumsted. Harriett Riley, "a masculine looking woman", was accused of assaulting Michael Lavin who appeared somewhat the worse for wear with a bandage around his head and obviously in a weak condition. With little evidence to hear and fearing for the welfare of Lavin the magistrates decided to remand Riley to appear before the Penkridge magistrates, Lord Hatherton and F.C. Percy Esq., on the following Monday, November 11th.

Harriett Riley, a single woman, who resided at Stafford, was brought from the custody cells and stood in the dock charged with stabbing Michael Lavin, a labourer, and also of assaulting Sergeant Upton of Cannock Police. The appearance of the accused when brought into court was wild and aggressive and "to say that her look was an impertinent one was only mildly describing it".

The first witness was Michael Lavin who lodged at the house of the prisoner's father in Mill Street, Cannock. He said that on Saturday, November 2nd he was at his lodgings at about 3.00 p.m. when the prisoner came in and asked him where her father and mother were. He told her that her mother had gone to America some two or three months ago and that he was lodging there to keep her father company. Her father was at work at Leacroft Colliery and would be home later. The prisoner then asked him to fetch her some ale as she had walked all the way from Stafford and she was very thirsty. He fetched a quart of ale from the Black Horse Hotel.

23. Mill Street (1920).

At about 3.30 p.m. her father came home from work and the three of them drank together. They had three more quarts of ale fetched in during the evening. About 8.00 p.m. her father asked the witness to go with him to fetch some groceries and they took the prisoner with them. They returned between nine and ten and then had another quart of ale. The prisoner's father then said it was time for bed and said that he and the witness would sleep upstairs and his daughter downstairs on the sofa. Before he went upstairs the prisoner's father said that he could not see his watch which should have been in a box on the table. The witness told him that his daughter had been wearing it since she came to the house. The prisoner denied it and accused the witness of taking it.

After some conversation the witness sat down on a chair and was taking his boots off when the prisoner sprang at him with a pocket knife in her right hand and stabbed him several times in quick succession in the head. He felt the blood pouring down his face and so grabbed the prisoner round the legs, pulled her down and wrenched the knife out of her hand. Her father, who was lying on the sofa, got up and helped the witness get loose from her. He then managed to get to the door and asked her father to get his boots as he would soon bleed to death. He then went to Sergeant Upton who took him to Dr. Butter to have his wounds dressed. He was then taken to Cannock Workhouse to recover.

At that point he was questioned by the prisoner (usual procedure at the time) and she accused him of striking her first and trying to indecently assault her. Both accusations he hotly denied.

The next witness was William Edwards, a miner who lived in Mill Street and the father of the prisoner. He said that when he returned from work on November 2nd he found his daughter in his house. He had not seen her for two or three years and he did not know why she had come. Lavin was also there and there was beer on the table and so they all had a drink. Michael Lavin sent the prisoner for three or four more quarts of ale during the evening. They then went for groceries and returned between nine and ten o'clock.

He then lay on the sofa and went to sleep. Shortly afterwards he woke and then missed his watch which had been in his vest pocket. He asked Lavin if he had got it and he said that he had not, but said that his daughter had it. At that point a quarrel broke out between Lavin and his daughter, but he tried to ignore it and went back to sleep. It was not long after that that he was awoken by Lavin shouting, *"William! William!"* He jumped up from the sofa and witnessed Lavin and his daughter down together on the floor struggling. Lavin was covered with blood and there was a bit of blood on the floor.

Shown the pocket knife produced as evidence Edwards said it was his knife and used for cutting tobacco when down the mine. (Miners often bought unrefined tobacco, rather like liquorice pieces, and sliced bits off to chew when down the pit. It helped to prevent coal dust from clogging their lungs. Once the juices were flowing from the chewing they could spit them out along with the dust hopefully.) He said it was kept in a box on the window sill when he was at home. He had used it after he got home that day, but there was no blood on it at that time.

Again Harriett questioned the witness who had to admit that he did not see the knife in her hand.

William Reeves, a grinder who also lived in Mill Street, testified that he was called to Edwards' house on November 2nd at about 11.30 p.m. by Sergeant Upton. He accompanied the sergeant upstairs where they found the prisoner lying on the bed. She had her clothes on but not her boots. The sergeant then told her that he had come to arrest her for stabbing Lavin and asked her to accompany him downstairs. Once they were downstairs the prisoner said, *"Let me put my boots on."* She then sat down by the fire and took up one boot as if going to put it on. Sergeant Upton stood in front of her and asked her several times to put her boots on. The prisoner then shook her father and said, *"Do you see who is here?"* and pointed to the officer.

Suddenly, without the slightest hesitation, she struck Sergeant Upton a blow on his face with the heel of her boot which she had in her right hand. The blow knocked the sergeant's helmet across the room and it was then that the witness noticed that the sergeant's face was bleeding from a wound over the right eye. The prisoner became very violent and he had to help the sergeant take her to the station.

Sergeant Upton told the court that Michael Lavin came to Cannock Police Station at about 10.55 p.m. on Saturday, November 2nd. He was bleeding badly from wounds in his head and complained of being stabbed. The witness examined his head, applied wet cloths and then took him to Dr. Butter's surgery. He then went to Mill Street in search of the prisoner. Once there he found the door locked. He knocked several times, but having got no answer he pushed the door open. Once inside he discovered blood on the floor and also spots on a wall. He also found the knife produced in court on the floor near to the fireplace. It was open and covered in blood and there was a light coloured hair on the blade - Lavin's hair colour.

Having got the assistance of William Reeves, the next door neighbour, they went upstairs and found the prisoner lying on the bed. He told her he wanted her to come downstairs as he wanted her for stabbing Michael Lavin. She came downstairs and sat by the fire where her boots were. She got one of the boots and then said to her father, *"They are going to arrest me for what I have done to that b----- for stealing your watch."* She then struck me over the left eye with the boot, cutting my eyebrow. The wound had to be dressed and stitched by Dr. Butter later.

The prisoner was taken to the police station with the help of Mr. Reeves. When she was charged she said, *"He (Lavin) should not have taken my father's watch. He thought of taking it and laying it on me. When I accused him with it he said, "You b----- flamer, I will blind you." He then struck at me and the knife was in my hand. I put up my hand to defend myself. I did not stab him with it."*

The final witness was Dr. John Kerr Butter who stated that at about 11.00 p.m. on the Saturday evening Sergeant Upton brought Lavin to his surgery to have some wounds dressed on his head. He examined him and found his head, face and the front part of his vest and shirt saturated with blood, which was spurting and welling out of four clean cut and punctured wounds on his head. The largest wound was above and behind the right ear measuring three inches long and extending through the scalp and down to the skull, severing a small artery. Just above that were two other wounds going down to the bone. The final wound was on the top of the head over the left eye, again down to the bone.

Dr. Butter said that Lavin was very faint due to the loss of blood and it was his opinion that the wounds were dangerous to life. They might have been caused by the knife produced in court. He had examined it the same day and found it wet with blood. He also testified that on the same evening he had tended Sergeant Upton and dressed his wound.

After all the evidence had been heard Harriett Riley pleaded not guilty to the charge of stabbing Michael Lavin, but guilty to the assault on Sergeant Upton. She was, however, committed to stand trial at the Stafford Assizes on both charges.

On Saturday December 14th Harriett Riley was charged with both offences before Mr. Justice Stephens. Having heard all the evidence the jury found her GUILTY of stabbing Michael Lavin, but the case of wounding Sergeant Upton was not pressed. It probably would have been had the first verdict not gone against her. It turned out that Harriett had previous convictions against her, including two for unlawfully wounding. The judge in his summing up said that she was not only "an habitual drunkard, but also an extremely passionate, violent woman". Taking into consideration that she had previously been convicted for a similar offence he would send her to gaol for eighteen months hard labour.

On hearing her sentence Harriett Riley impudently replied to the judge, *"You're a grand old man."* Despite the solemnity of the occasion the onlookers could not help but laugh out loud as she was led from the dock.

The final case is one with which today's public are only too familiar, that of drink-driving.

Historical Note: - In 1872 it became an offence to be drunk whilst in charge of carriages, horses, cattle or steam engines. In 1925 the Criminal Justice Act made it an offence to be drunk in charge of any mechanically propelled vehicle on the highway or in a public place. The fine could be £50 or 4 months in prison and disqualification from driving for a year. In 1930 the Road Traffic Act made it an offence to drive "whilst under the influence of drink or a drug to such an extent as to be incapable of having proper control of the vehicle". In 1967 the Road Safety Act introduced the Legal Drink Drive Limit.

Just before 7.00 p.m. on the evening of May 11th, 1934 Mary Jervis, aged twenty three, left her home in Bridge Cross, Chase Terrace and drove to Chasetown Police Station to pick up her friend, Mrs. Cresswell, who worked at the police station. She then drove to Hednesford and called in at the Bridge Inn, Hightown where she had two bottles of beer. Having left there she drove to Milford and then back to Cannock to the Railway Inn where between 8.30 p.m. and 9.00 p.m. she had another bottle of beer and a gin. The couple then went towards Norton Canes and called in at the Holly Bush where Mary had another two bottles of beer and a gin. They finished up at the Fleur de Lys where she had a further half a glass of gin.

Having left the last public house she proceeded to drive home and whilst going through Bridgtown she collided with a cyclist, Jesse Edgington, and injured him so seriously that he was in hospital for six weeks. Not realising that she had hit anyone, she continued to drive home and on reaching the Wooden Stables, near Biddulph's Pool, she collided with and fatally injured another person. Thomas Landers, a pedlar from Welshpool, was hit with such force that he died instantly. Again she did not realise she had hit anyone and continued on her way. When reaching Sankey's Corner she hit another cyclist, Charles Shorthose, and knocked him off his cycle. Amazingly she was still unaware that anything had happened and drove home and went to bed.

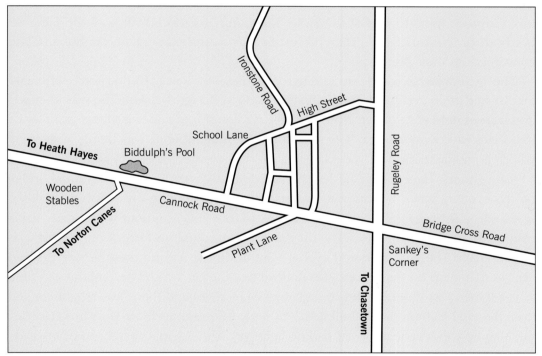

24. Map of Chase Terrace 1902.

At 2.20 a.m. on the morning of May 12th the police called at Mary's home. She was in bed, but came downstairs when called by her mother. Whilst waiting for her Police Constable Littlewood examined her car and discovered the damaged headlamp and running board. Superintendent Jeffery told her he was making enquiries about an accident in Bridgtown and that he understood she had been out driving. She admitted that she had been around Milford way, but she had not called anywhere. He then told her that he had already spoken to Mrs. Cresswell and after further questioning she was arrested and taken to the police station and charged.

After lengthy investigations and several appearances before local magistrates Mary Jervis was remanded to stand trial at Stafford Assizes on three charges, one of which included manslaughter. On Tuesday, July 3rd 1934 her trial, which would last two days, was presided over by Mr. Justice Mackinnon with Sir Reginald Coventry for the Prosecution and Mr. Arthur Ward for the Defence.

The case began with lengthy arguments on whether the manslaughter charge should be heard separately, Mr Ward arguing for separation of the three cases, his argument being that the two minor charges would prejudice the case of manslaughter if she were found guilty of them. The judge finally decided that all three cases should be heard together. That having been decided Sir Reginald outlined the case against Mary Jervis and then called the first witnesses, the landlords or landladies of the various public houses Mary had frequented on the evening of May 11th. They were Mrs. Eva Jones of the Bridge Inn, Hightown; Mr. Percy Curtiss of the Railway Inn, Cannock; Jane Kibble of the Holly Bush and Horatio Edwards of the Fleur de Lys both of Norton Canes. They all testified as to the amount of alcohol she had consumed on their premises.

The next witness was Jesse Edgington of Rugeley Road, Hednesford, who said that he had been cycling along the Walsall Road at Bridgtown when he was knocked down from behind by a car. Unfortunately he could remember nothing more as he had blacked out soon after. The next thing he remembered was being in hospital where he remained for six weeks.

John Thomas Haycock of Cheslyn Hay said that he was cycling towards Churchbridge on the evening when he saw two cyclists and a lorry coming towards him. He then saw a car which was travelling at about thirty to forty miles an hour without any lights coming up behind the cyclists. The car did not alter course and struck one cyclist with a loud crash. The light coloured cyclist went up in the air and then he saw the two cyclists in a heap on the ground. He noticed that the car was a Ford and he was able to get some of its number. The street lamps were alight and there was a light coming from the Drill Hall on the Walsall Road. In reply to questions from Mr. Ward Haycock said that he was sure that the car had no lights on. Also Edgington did come alongside the other cyclist (two abreast) at the time of the accident.

James Cliffe of Bridgtown said that he was opposite the Drill Hall when the accident happened. He heard the crash and noticed that the car had no lights on. It was being driven in a zigzag manner and at a fast pace. After the crash he got into the road to attract the driver's attention, but the car did not stop. He shouted *"Stop"* as loud as he could and then took the car number.

Cyril Thomas Rushton of Walsall Road, Bridgtown said that he also heard a crash and dashed out and found a man lying in the road four feet from the gutter. He crushed a cigarette where the cyclist's head was lying. Was there a suggestion that Edgington was smoking whilst cycling and so not fully paying attention to the road and traffic?

The next group of witnesses referred to the two later accidents which happened at the Wooden Stables and Chase Terrace. Sidney Henry Parr of Chasetown said that he was walking from Heath Hayes to Sankey's Corner and was standing near the Wooden Stables when he heard a crash. He saw a dark saloon car travelling fast in a straight course towards Sankey's Corner and then saw a man who had been injured. No other car had passed him in the meantime.

Bernard George Brookes, also of Chasetown, said he was with Parr and he had gone into a house near the Wooden Stables to have a cycle repaired. While he was there he heard a noise and noticed a small car go by which was going fast.

Unfortunately neither of the last two witnesses actually saw the accident at the Wooden Stables and so their evidence might be construed as hearsay, but the next witness was actually present at the third accident. William Cantrell of Chasetown said that he was motor cycling along Ironstone Road and as he neared the junction of Ironstone Road and Cannock Road he got off and pushed his machine. He then saw a car travelling on the wrong side of the road and it remained on the wrong side until it was just sixteen feet from him. It came within inches of him. He let go of his motor cycle and jumped into the porch of a nearby house. The car had only one light on and it was a blue saloon car. There were two or three cyclists nearer Sankey's Corner. One cycle was black and one white and they were on the proper side of the road. He then heard a crash and saw that the car had struck the offside cyclist (Shorthose).

Thomas Rock, a miner from Chasetown, said that a car passed him fifty yards before it struck the cyclist (Shorthose). The car got very close to the curb on the left hand side and then went into the centre of the road and struck Shorthose. It then just carried on up the road.

Charles Derry Shorthose of Burntwood Road, Hammerwich said that he was cycling near Sankey's Corner when a car came up behind. He mentioned the car to a cyclist who was with him and the next thing he knew was that he had been knocked down.

So much for the two cyclists knocked off their cycles, but what of the fatal accident which killed sixty eight year old Thomas Landers. Unlike the previous two accidents there were no actual witnesses, but the police did recover vital evidence from the car. Constable Littlewood said that he went to the Wooden Stables and found Landers lying on the footpath on his correct side of the road. His cap was found fifty eight feet from the body and there were several pieces of broken glass on the footpath. Constable Wedge was with him when he found a piece of glass a few feet from the body.

25. The Wooden
    Stables area,
    Chase Terrace.

The constable then went on to say that he went to the home of Mary Jervis at 2.20 a.m. on May 12th. She was in bed at the time, but came down when requested. He saw her car and the headlamp's glass was smashed. He collected the pieces and also some of the running board. He then added that Superintendent Jeffery had told the accused that he was making enquiries about an accident at Bridgtown and he understood that she had been out with her car. She admitted that and said that she had driven around Milford with a friend, but they had not called anywhere. At that point the superintendent told her that he had already spoken to Mrs. Cresswell. He also told her that two men had been injured at Bridgtown, one had been killed at the Wooden Stables and some cyclists injured at Chasetown.

The constable then told the court that the accused said, *"Bridgtown? I don't know where it is."* She, however, said that she remembered striking a motor cyclist at the Wooden Stables as she had heard a thud. She also remembered touching two cyclists at Sankey's Corner, but she had not stopped as she had not thought it was much. The constable said that she began to make a statement, but after giving a few particulars asked if it was compulsory. When told that it was not she said, *"I don't think I will make one."*

When she accompanied the constable, the superintendent and her father to the garage to inspect her car she said, *"This is my little flivver. You don't think it would kill a man, do you?"* to which her father replied, *"Don't talk so utterly ridiculous."* The constable then said that he and the superintendent inspected the car and found blood and hair on the nearside handle. He had found hairs on the glass found near Landers' body and the two were matched later. There were also wheel marks on the side of the body facing Heath Hayes and they too matched the accused's car. He had also found tyre marks at the scene where it had mounted the path for a short distance.

Inspector Swain, who had also gone to the accident scene, told how he had found a piece of glass fifteen yards from Landers' head. When he had questioned her at the station she had said that she remembered touching a motor cyclist at the Wooden Stables and also two at Sankey's Corner. She had added that the cyclists at

Sankey's Corner were riding abreast and that they should not be allowed to do so.

In reply to questions from Mr. Ward the inspector said that a statement had been taken from Mrs. Cresswell, but when they revisited her to verify some details they could not see her because she was being interviewed by a solicitor for the Defence.

Superintendent Jeffery then gave evidence and stated that the pieces of glass found close to the body fitted into two pieces of glass found on the car in the garage. They were then passed over to the judge and jury who were satisfied that they did indeed fit together. The superintendent then stated that he mentioned to the accused that she had not stopped after the crash and she said, *"I was in a hurry. It was getting late."* When he arrested her she said, *"What can I say. I don't know the man Landers at all."*

At that point, as it was getting late in the day and the Prosecution had finished its case, the judge halted proceedings to continue the following day. Before Mr. Ward could start his case for the Defence on the Wednesday the jury left the court to inspect the car which was in the outer hall. Once they had resumed their seats Mr. Ward began by telling the jury that if they decided on a verdict of manslaughter against his client they must be certain that she was criminally negligent and had a reckless regard for the safety of life and limb for other users of the road. He stated that the accused could not argue with the facts that she had caused the death of Landers and injured both Shorthose and Edgington and they and their families should receive damages and she was willing to pay those.

He then proceeded to say that anybody who drove a car would appreciate that for a person to drive recklessly and criminally they would not be in their right mind and he was going to prove that about his client. At that point he was interrupted by the judge who asked, *"Are you asking for a verdict of guilty, but insane?"* Mr. Ward replied, *"No, my lord, you will soon see what I am coming to."* He continued saying that his client was a timid and anxious character who was kindly, but suffered terribly at times from depression. (The jury had three women in it and it was to those that he directed his attention, hoping for their sympathy.) At such periods, he continued, she was hysterical and owing to its pressure she would often go into a form of trance. It was that that had happened during the accidents. Mrs. Creswell had been ill and out of the goodness of her own heart his client had taken her for a drive to cheer her up, despite feeling ill herself.

During the journey his client was in great pain and the calls at the various inns were to alleviate that pain. Her illness was the cause of the accidents. As to her drunkenness Mr. Ward stated that no person could be so drunk as to drive in the manner described and then sober enough at 10.30 p.m. to drive safely into a garage.

Having made his argument Mary Jervis was called to the witness box. She said that she had promised to take Mrs. Cresswell out on May 11th and, despite her mother asking her not to go as she was ill, she did not want to disappoint her friend. They first drove to the Bridge Inn at Hightown where she had two small beers. They then drove towards Milford, but she was in a lot of pain and so Mrs. Cresswell suggested they call at the Shrewsbury Arms, Rugeley. There she had a gin for the pain, but when she left she was still in pain and so they headed for home. However, on the way they called at the Railway Inn, Cannock and there she asked for a certain gin which she thought would alleviate the pain. As they had not got that type she had another.

Still on the way home they called at the Holly Bush, Norton Canes to see if they had the special gin, but they did not have it. All the time the pain in her stomach was getting worse, like cramp, and so they called at the Fleur de Lys, but she could not recollect much of that visit, except the man said they were just in time. She then went on to say that she had no recollection of seeing a cyclist. It was as if it were a dream and she did not remember any accident at all. She had a vague recollection of feeling a thud at the Wooden Stables and thought it was a motor cyclist, but did not know why she had not stopped. Again she only vaguely remembered the cyclist at Sankey's Corner, but did not think anything had happened. She said that she had told the police that she had not stopped anywhere on the drive because she was frightened.

26. Sankey's Corner c.1940. (The Jervis family kept the cinema on the corner.)

In reply to questioning by Sir Reginald she said that she was not accustomed to having alcohol, but she had been advised to drink gin, but no one had told her to drink beer. She did not think that what she had on that night was overcoming her. When asked why she went out that night when feeling ill she replied that she had promised Mrs. Cresswell and did not want to upset her. As to the amount that she drank on the evening she said that she only had three bottles of beer the whole night, but could not remember how many gins. However, she did not know how she got home that evening or if she had the car light on.

When she got into the garage she noticed a car lamp was damaged and so she telephoned Mrs. Cresswell. She told her there must have been an accident and asked her to inform Police Constable Cresswell about it. Finally she said that she was not in the habit of getting drunk as her parents were very strict, adding that she was deeply sorry for what had happened.

Isabel Jervis, Mary's mother, referring to her daughter's illness, said that she had gone into a kind of trance three or four times before and when like that she was vacant and did not answer when spoken to. On the night in question she had begged her daughter not to drive and she hoped that her daughter would never be allowed to drive again. When she got home that night she was very pale and looked like a corpse, but did not smell of drink. Her father, not realising her condition, upbraided her for being late.

Miles Jervis, her father, said that his daughter was a bit dazed when she came home that night, but did not smell of drink. He told the court that he thought his daughter had been led into taking the drink. Lilian Bailey said that she had known the accused for four years and had known her to be very ill on occasions. In fact she was ill on May 9th.

With the Defence witnesses finished Mr. Ward stated that there was one vital witness who had not been called, Mrs. Cresswell, who could have told them all about the incidents. He dared the Prosecution to call her saying that they would not. It was not his duty as Defence lawyer, but it was the duty of the Prosecution to call all witnesses whether for or against, but they would not as one of their witnesses was Constable Cresswell. In response Sir Reginald said, *"The Prosecution did not call all witnesses, but only those whom they could rely on to tell the truth."*

Once the lawyers had finished their arguments Judge Mackinnon summed up the case, clarifying the position on negligence for the jury. As for the accuser's illness which might render her in a type of trance and so making it a case of wanton driving (a lesser crime) he said that *"it would have been more satisfactory if it had been supported by medical evidence"*. The jury then retired to consider their verdict, but an hour later they returned to say that they could not agree. After giving them further advice they finally returned with a verdict after another one and a half hours. Their verdict was GUILTY on all three charges, but with a strong recommendation to mercy.

The judge then sentenced Mary Jervis to six months imprisonment. When asked if she had anything to say Mary Jervis pleaded, *"Oh, please don't send me to prison."* The judge replied that he had reduced his intended sentence because of the jury's plea for mercy. At that she collapsed and had to be held up by wardresses. Her mother also collapsed and had to be assisted from the court. Several relatives and friends also burst into tears.

MATRICIDE AND FRATRICIDE
Penkridge and Churchbridge

One of the strongest bonds in human nature is that between parents and their children. Let anyone dare try to come between them and all hell will usually break loose. For that reason it is extremely difficult to believe that that relationship could somehow be destroyed and yet occasionally it is, at times resulting in tragedy. As the American rhyme goes, "Lizzie Borden took and axe and gave her father forty whacks. When she saw what she had done she gave her mother forty one." But exactly what caused Lizzie Borden to explode was never fully explained at her trail. The following cases also have that strange air of mystery and sadness about them.

Life had been particularly hard for the young Stone boy (his Christian name was never given during the proceedings because he was only fourteen). He had lost his mother at such an early age that he could not even remember her. His father, Thomas, had remarried, but once again his second wife died early when the lad was only ten years old. The lad's step-sister had left to go into service and his step-brother had also left. Seemingly bitter at his fate Thomas Stone took it out on the lad, frequently shouting and swearing at him and also beating him. His behaviour towards the boy had been so bad that at one time an Inspector for the Prevention of Cruelty to Children had called to warn Thomas about his conduct towards the boy. It was clear to everyone who knew the pair that the lad was terrified of his father.

It was in that powder-keg situation that the events of September 28th, 1937 took place. Told that they were going to leave their cottage (Mitton Cottages, Penkridge) in a few days the lad was told to help with the packing. As usual the boy was being picked on and in danger of getting another beating when a neighbour called. On leaving the lad in the attic Thomas said that he would deal with him later. Panic and fear must have overtaken the little lad because he loaded the gun which his father kept and shot Thomas as the neighbour was leaving. Stunned and quaking with fear the lad simply raced to neighbours for them to fetch a doctor. Thomas never recovered and the lad was brought before a special court at Cannock on Wednesday 15th, October accused of the murder of his father. All the witnesses who were neighbours would relate the same sorry story of the lad's ill-treatment and fear.

Mrs. Elizabeth Moore of Stretton said that she had first cleaned for the father in 1934 when he lived at Church Eaton and subsequently did most of the housework when Thomas and his son moved to Mitton Cottages. When she did not go to the cottage the lad was forced to do the housework. She had been told by Thomas that he and his son were leaving on September 29th to go to live in Birmingham, but the lad was not happy about the move. On September 27th there had been some trouble between Thomas and his son. The two were trying to pack some bedsteads and the lad was having difficulty managing the heavy bedstead.

Mrs. Moore told the hearing that she was downstairs ironing, but Thomas's shouting and bad language was so bad that she went upstairs fearful that Thomas would harm the lad. When she got to the upstairs landing Thomas was just "landing out" at the lad and so she got in between them, pushed the boy towards his bedroom for his own safety and said to Thomas, *"I will help with the bedsteads."*

When questioned about Thomas's behaviour towards the lad she said that Thomas was a big man and nearly six feet tall. He had continually bullied the lad who was small for his age. The lad was terrified of his father who was always shouting at him and had "shown him no kindness". If the boy did not do things exactly right Thomas would shout at him and she even heard him say that he would knock his b----- head off and show him what was for. She always tried to get in between them as she knew Thomas would strike the lad. She had witnessed him hitting the lad on several occasions and the lad took it very hard. As far as she was concerned the lad was "very quiet, reserved and well behaved". She also knew that the N.S.P.C.C. had called about Thomas's behaviour towards the boy.

She also said that the boy had a step-sister and the fact that he was corresponding with her caused trouble because Thomas thought that she was trying to turn the lad against him.

When questioned about the gun Mrs. Moore stated that it hung on two nails on the wall between the clock and a little box and opposite the window and was within easy reach of anyone. She had never examined it and could not say whether it was loaded or not. As far as she knew the lad had never used the gun.

The next witness was Colonel Charles Playfair of Great Barr, a gun expert, who told the court it was a double barrelled sporting type. The right barrel was not working owing to a mechanical fault, but the left was in perfect working order. He had tested it and the spread of a shot from seven feet was one inch. He said that if the gun was fired to within three feet three inches of a body the shot would follow the line of the barrel. Thomas's wound proved that the lad had been very close when he fired the gun.

Dr. David Hill of Gnosall said that he was called to the cottage and saw Stone lying on the kitchen floor. He was dying from a gunshot wound to the lower abdomen. He dressed the wound as far as he could and then ordered Stone's removal to Stafford General Infirmary. In reply to questions Dr. Hill said that he was the Stones regular doctor and had seen quite a lot of the lad. As far as he was concerned the boy was quite reserved, well-behaved and perfectly "normal".

Dr. Charles Reid of Stafford said that he had carried out the post mortem and found the cause of death to be due to shock which was secondary to severe haemorrhage caused by the gunshot wound. Stone had been five feet eight inches tall and the shot was three feet six inches from his feet.

Sidney Charles Jackson, a farm labourer of Mitton Lodge Cottages, Penkridge said that he had called at Stone's cottage at 7.45 p.m. on September 28th for two walking sticks which Stone had promised to his father. Stone gave him the walking sticks and they talked for about ten minutes. Stone then accompanied him down the path about half way and then turned back towards the cottage. The witness then got on his bicycle and went to ride off when he heard a gunshot. He then heard Stone say, *"Oh, Sid, he has shot me in the guts."* The witness ran back up the pathway and saw Stone with a hand on each side of the door frame, facing the cottage. He put his arms out to save Stone from falling and lowered him to the ground. As he was doing this the lad came through the door. At Stone's request he went to a farm for help and then returned to the cottage, meeting another man on the way. The farmer, Mr. Stanton, arrived and Stone was moved into the living room and placed on the floor.

Under questioning Jackson stated that he had not gone into the house that night nor had he spoken to the lad. Also he did not speak to the lad as he ran passed him, nor did the lad speak. When he got to the farm the lad had already been there and had arranged for a doctor to be telephoned for. When he got back to Stone's cottage and helped carry him inside he saw the gun on the kitchen floor. It was lying near the corner of the table. He also stated that he heard no conversation between Stone and the lad before the shot was fired. Finally, he said that he had known the lad for about seven or eight weeks.

Roland Embury of Mitton Farm said that he was walking in some fields near Mitton Cottages about three or four hundred yards away when he heard a shot from the direction of the cottages. He heard a man cry out, *"Oh, my God, he has shot me!"* It sounded like Stone's voice and he went to the gate where he met Jackson and they went to the cottage together. On the way, about seven or eight minutes after the shot, he asked Jackson what was the matter and he told him what had happened. He did not see the lad until later, about dusk.

Edith Stanton of Lower Mitton Farm said that at about 7.45 p.m. there was a knock at the back door and on opening it she saw the boy. He was very agitated and was wringing his hands and seemed as if he could not speak. She had asked, *"Whatever do you want at this time of day?"* and he replied, *"Get the doctor quick. I have shot my dad."* She took the lad into the kitchen and asked him where his father was and if he was hurt. He simply replied, *"Get the doctor quick. I want the doctor."* She then told him that she would have to telephone the police if he had shot his father, but he did not reply. She then telephoned the police and asked them to get a doctor.

She then said that she was with the lad for a quarter of an hour and he said, *"I hope the doctor comes quick. Suppose my father should die."* She then told the court that she asked the lad what made him do it and he said that his father was always grumbling at him and he could not stand it any longer. He also said that he had lost control over himself. He said that he did not know where they were going the next morning and he had been upset about the leaving.

When questioned Mrs. Stanton said that she had known the boy since he came to the village and he was not a boy to show a vicious temper. He was a nice, quiet lad and very well liked by everyone. He was so distraught and anxious about the whole business that she telephoned the doctor a second time.

George Henry Stanton, Edith's husband, told the court that he was standing near his farm buildings at 7.45 p.m. when the boy ran to the house. He followed him and when he entered he heard the boy say that he had shot his dad. He asked the lad if it had been an accident and he replied, *"No, I shot him."* George then said that he went to the cottage and saw Stone who called him over and made a statement. When he saw the boy later he asked him why he had done it and the lad said that his father was always on to him and ill-using him.

In reply to questioning George stated that it was common knowledge in the village that the father had ill-used the lad for months. During his conversation with the boy after the affair he said that the lad *"seemed to be in a pitiable condition. He was wringing his hands and the look on his face I shall never forget as long as I live. He was not in a condition to know what he was doing or saying. I have heard his father using language to him that was not fit to put on paper."*

John Birchall of Woodside Farm, Stretton said that he accompanied George Stanton home and saw the lad. He asked him if he had used the gun before and he said that he had not. He did admit to having a sporting gun which he used for rabbiting. He did not ask the lad any more as the boy was so distressed.

The final witness was Police Sergeant Hulse of Gnosall. He said that he went to the cottage and saw the father and accompanied him to the hospital. He then returned to Mitton and arrested the lad at Stanton's Farm. He cautioned him at the station and charged him with the murder of his father. The lad then made a statement which said, *"Ever since my mother died he has grumbled at me and knocked me about. The inspector of cruelty came to him once. I was on edge with moving home. He then started grumbling at me again and shouting. I lost my head and got the gun and shot him. I heard my father shout so I dropped the gun and ran to the nearest telephone. I loaded the gun myself."* When questioned the sergeant said that the lad was not in a distressed state when he saw him.

The magistrates had no alternative but to charge the lad with murder and send him to gaol to await the Assizes. When he was charged he simply said, *"I am not guilty. I reserve my defence."* (Obviously the lad had been told exactly what to say by Mr. Cooper, his Defence Counsel.)

The case began at the Assize Court in Stafford on November 25th, 1937 before Mr. Justice Finlay. Mr. A.W. Copeland appeared for the Prosecution and Mr. Thorneycroft for the Defence. Every witness called at the magistrate's court reappeared and again told their sad stories about the father's treatment of the lad and the fatal events of September 28th. Finally it was the turn of the young lad to give his account of the affair.

He stated the following: - He had once lived at Church Eaton. He did not remember his own mother, but had a step-mother, who had died when he was ten; a step-sister who had gone into service; and a step-brother who had also left. When he was twelve he and his father went into lodgings for about ten weeks and then went to Mitton Cottages. On days when Mrs. Moore did not come he did the housework.

Shortly after his last birthday of fourteen he left school and went to work in Stafford at an engineering works. He stayed there until September 25th when he left. His father had given him a sealed letter for the timekeeper some time before, but he did not know its contents. Only a week after did he find out that he was to leave as his father had decided that they were moving, but without telling him.

On September 27th he was helping his father in the attic packing a bedstead, but he could not keep it straight. His father swore at him and was going to hit him but Mrs. Moore intervened and he went to bed. He stayed there for the rest of the day because his father had gone out and he knew that if he were still up when his father returned he would give him a "good hiding". On September 28th he had cooked the dinner and in the afternoon his father was again swearing at him as he was clearing up the garden. Mr. Jackson then came and his father said, *"You wait until Mr. Jackson's been and I'll deal with you. For two pins I would knock your head off."*

He continued: - *"I heard father shouting good night. He started to come back. I was frightened and got the gun."* Just as he came in the door he said, *"Now you little b---- I'll deal with you." The gun just went off."* Mr. Thorneycroft then asked, *"Did you aim the gun at your father?"* to which the lad replied, *"No."*

There then followed cross-examination by the counsellors and the judge as follows: -

Judge: - *Did you load the gun?*

Lad: - *I must have done, but I can't remember. I must have done because father never left it loaded.*

Mr. Thorneycroft: - *Why did you get the gun? What were you going to do with it?*

Lad: - *I was going to hit out with it if he came at me.*

Mr. Thorneycroft: - *Did you intend to shoot your father?*

Lad: - *No.*

In reply to Mr. Copeland the lad said that it was an accident. He did not remember saying it was an accident. He remembered talking to the Stantons, but did not remember what he said to them. He did remember saying that he had shot his father.

He remembered being taken to the station and signing a statement.

Mr. Copeland: - *You did load the gun?*

Lad: - *I must have done.*

Mr. Copeland: - *What for?*

Lad: - *I don't know. I don't remember doing it.*

Mr. Copeland: - *Wasn't it because you meant to shoot your father?*

Lad: - *No, sir.*

Mr. Copeland: - *He had said he would deal with you and for two pins knock your head off?*

Lad: - *Yes.*

Mr. Copeland: - *It was not the first time he had said that?*

Lad: - *No, sir.*

Mr. Copeland: - *He never did it, did he?*

Lad: - *No, but I thought he would do it that night as he said he would chuck me in the brook and clear off alone.*

Judge: - *Is it a deep brook?*

Lad: - *Yes, and I cannot swim.*

Judge: - *When did he say that?*

Lad: - *On the Tuesday night just before Mr. Jackson came.*

Mr. Copeland: - *Was that why you took the gun?*

Lad: - *Yes.*

Having finished that cross-examination both Counsels summed up their cases. Mr. Copeland questioned why the lad had changed his statement to accidental shooting, but had to admit that the lad was a bundle of nerves. However, he did admit to loading the gun. Strangely for a prosecuting counsel he finished by saying that he only wished that they could reduce the case (meaning from murder to manslaughter), but that was up to the judge. Mr. Thorneycroft argued for a verdict of not guilty saying to the jury that if they believed that the lad "petrified with fear, picked up the gun and it went off by accident he was entitled to a verdict of not guilty". He then vividly painted a picture of a terrified lad, trembling with fear, holding a gun waiting for the "good hiding" that he knew would happen as soon as Mr. Jackson left. *"The boy might have blindly fired in sheer terror, or it might be that in the hands of a trembling boy the gun went off accidentally."*

In his summing up the judge said that there was no doubt that the lad had killed his father. If the jury believed the Prosecution that at the time there was no provocation to justify the prisoner firing the gun then it might be that a verdict of manslaughter would be correct. If they believed the Defence about the accidental firing, of which there was "some difficulty" or if they thought the lad acted in self-defence then the firing of the gun might be held to be justified and a verdict of not guilty would be correct.

It took the jury just twenty minutes to decide on a verdict of NOT GUILTY. The lad was discharged and Mr. Thorneycroft said that arrangements had been made for his future. Those arrangements were not disclosed.

The next case follows a similar pattern – a young lad, none too clever, dominated by a bullying father.

John Arthur Douglas, aged 39, and his wife, Dora Elizabeth, aged 45, had not long moved into No. 5 Leacroft Lane, Churchbridge, by April 1956, but sufficient enough for the neighbours to realise that something was dreadfully wrong when neither had been seen since Sunday April 15th. Having informed the police on Tuesday April 17th about their concerns Sergeant O'Neil, who knew the couple, was sent to investigate. Not able to gain access to the property he looked through the bungalow window and saw two bodies lying on the bed. He immediately broke into the house and discovered that both had been shot and were obviously dead. The coroner, having been informed, the bodies were removed to the mortuary at Mount Pleasant, Cheslyn Hay to be examined by Professor J.M. Webster, pathologist.

27. 5 Leacroft Road, Churchbridge.

There were, however, several mysteries about the affair – Hubert Douglas, the victim's sixteen year old son, was missing as was the family car. Cannock Police did not have long to wait to solve both. Later the same they were contacted by Rugeley Police who had Hubert in their custody. Detective Sergeant Hulme was dispatched and at 3.00 p.m. he brought Hubert back to Cannock Police Station. At 4.15 p.m. the same afternoon he appeared before a special juvenile court before Mr. H.W. Cornes and about fifteen of the press. Mr. Alexander, the Clerk, warned the press about restrictions regarding publicity and then young Hubert Douglas was brought in through a private entrance. Superintendent F. Wall stated that the police were not sufficiently in a position to proceed with the charge and asked for a remand until April 25th.

The coroner, however, wished the case to begin and so Detective Sergeant Hulme told the hearing that he had brought the lad back to Cannock from Rugeley and once there had informed him that he was being held in connection with two people. He told him that he had been to No.5 Leacroft Lane and seen the bodies and believed that the lad knew something about their deaths, to which the lad had said, *"What can I say, except that I done it?"*

Police Sergeant O'Neil told the hearing that he knew both victims personally. John Douglas was a metal dealer and Dora Douglas was a housewife.

Professor Webster testified that he first saw both bodies at their home on April 17th in the double bed and then had the corpses removed to Cheslyn Hay Mortuary where he examined them. He concluded that each of them had died from shock and haemorrhage due to the passage of a point two-two bullet through the brain. Both had been healthy people before their deaths which happened in the early hours of April 15th.

At that point in the proceedings the coroner adjourned the juvenile court to allow the police to further their investigations. He also issued certificates to allow Mr. James Douglas of Old Hall Farm, Great Wyrley to arrange for the burial of his brother and sister-in-law. The couple were buried at Aldridge on Saturday, April 21st. A brief inquest on the deaths was held at Salem Schoolroom, Cheslyn Hay on April 18th before Mr. D.F. Cave just to identify the bodies and it was adjourned until a later date.

On May 9th 1956 Hubert Douglas was brought before Cannock Juvenile Court once more. The magistrate was Mr. C.L. Hotchkiss. First to give evidence was Professor Webster who stated that he had first examined the bodies at No. 5 Leacroft Lane and found the bedding to be saturated with blood. After having the bodies removed to the mortuary he conducted the post mortem on April 17th and the only mark of violence on the man was a bullet hole an inch above the right ear. He had recovered a 22 bullet from the brain. The woman had a hole two and a half inches from the right ear. In both cases there was an absence of blackening or burning proving the gunman had been a reasonable distance from the victims. There was no evidence of a struggle. The exact time of death was difficult to calculate as putrefaction had quickened due to the weight of bedding covering the bodies.

Chief Petty Officer Tuck of the Royal Navy Diving School, Chatham, stated that his unit had been requested to search the Serpentine in London to look for a gun. He and four of his men, after being given its rough location, finally discovered it and returned it to Cannock Police.

John Noden of Saredon Hall Cottages, Saredon said that he was at the bar of an inn on Saturday, April 14th when he noticed the accused with a man and a woman. He had joined them for a drink, but the lad just had lemonade. The three left the inn at about 9.40 p.m. He also stated that he had known John Douglas for a time and knew that he "liked a drink".

Ernest Enoch Sambrook of No.7 Leacroft Lane said that on April 14th he saw the car in the driveway of No.5. He noticed that the lights were on in the bungalow at 10.30 p.m. The following morning the car had gone. He also told the court that he had been the one who telephoned the police and said to them, *"We are worried about some people who came to live at No. 5 next door to us a short time ago. We have not seen them for two days. I have looked through the bedroom window and it seems as if there are two bodies lying on the bed with clothing piled on top of them."* Not long after the police arrived.

George Harold Sharpe of No. 3 Leacroft Lane said that at about 12.30 a.m. on the Sunday morning he saw the lights of a car next door and it appeared to be John

Douglas's car. The driver appeared to be backing out of the drive.

William Charles Carroll of Union Street, Rugeley told the court that on Tuesday April 17th he was at the Watch Tower on Rugeley Bank when he noticed the accused climbing a ladder seemingly to get into the tower. The young lad had a shotgun with him. He asked the lad if he had permission to be there and if he had permission to carry a gun. The lad told him he had permission for the gun. The witness then took him into the tower and the lad fired his gun through an open window. He then reloaded it and the witness told him that what he was doing was dangerous. At that point the lad gave up the gun and the witness took it and some cartridges and threw them through the window.

He then said to the lad, *"Have you done anything wrong?"* to which the accused replied, *"No one can do the harm I have done. I would willingly give my eyes to undo what I have done. I think you had better telephone Cannock Police."*

Instead the witness telephoned Rugeley Police and P.C. Lines was dispatched to the Tower. Once there he spoke to the lad, collected the gun from outside and searched the haversack which the lad had with him. Inside there was £52 17s 1d. He then escorted the lad to Rugeley Police Station. After telephoning Cannock Police the accused was transferred over there. Whilst in custody Hubert showed Cannock Police a map of the London area on which he marked the spot in the Serpentine where he had thrown the gun.

All witnesses now having given their evidence young Hubert Douglas was given the opportunity to have his say. Under guidance from Mr. Stretton, his Defence lawyer, he told the court that on Saturday evening April 14th he had been out with his parents to a public house and at about 9.30 p.m. they left and went home. His mother and father were quarrelling and he tried to stop them. His father was threatening the two of them with a gun into which he was loading bullets. After the quarrel stopped he took the gun to hide it from his father. His mother then shouted, *"Shoot him!"* meaning her husband and so he did. She then started screaming and he told her to be quiet. However, when she carried on screaming he shot her as well.

Mr. Stretton told the court that although the lad was by no means simple he nevertheless was educationally backward and could not read or write owing to his lack of schooling. For years he had had to help his father in the metal business, often missing his schooling.

At that point the magistrate closed the proceedings and young Hubert Douglas was transferred to Stafford Gaol to await trial at the Assizes. The case began on July 2nd, 1956. Mr. R.G. Mickelthwaite for the Prosecution said that the accused had taken his father's car and money and gone to London to dispose of the gun. He had returned to Rugeley and called the police saying that he was a next door neighbour and was worried about the people at No. 5 Leacroft Lane, Churchbridge. He said that he had looked through the window and had seen bodies on the bed. Counsel for the Prosecution insisted that the bodies could not be seen from the window and yet that was how the police had described seeing them. He was endeavouring to prove to the court that Hubert was not as "simple minded" as would be made out by the Defence. After his opening statement all the witnesses from the magistrate's court were heard, giving exactly the same evidence as before.

Mr. E. Ryder Richardson, Counsel for the Defence, knew that the only way to save his client from the severest of punishments was to keep insisting that Hubert was not fully responsible for his actions due to his lack of education and worldliness. In his statement Hubert stated that he could not read or write. He had helped his father in the metal business since he was twelve years old and rarely gone to school. He had run away from home at times because of the constant quarrelling between his parents. On one occasion he had stayed away for three days because he was blamed for the quarrelling.

On the night of the shooting he had tried to stop his parents from quarrelling, but his father had sent him to bed. During that quarrel his father had threatened to change the property into his own name and "chuck out" his mother and Hubert. Also during the quarrel his father had gone into the kitchen and Hubert had followed him and seen him loading a gun. He had got the gun from his father, but in a struggle his father got it back and threatened to "chuck" him out in the morning. His father then told him to go to bed.

Describing what had happened after he had gone to bed, Hubert said that he had remained fully clothed and just lay on the bed. He added, *"I waited until 12.45 a.m. and heard him snoring. I went into their bedroom to take the gun away. Mother was still awake because as I was taking the gun she said, "put the light on." I switched the light on and she said, "Shoot him. I can't move because he has got his legs over me." I then pointed the gun at father and she said, "Shoot! Shoot!" and so I fired at his head. Mother then screamed and would not stop and so I shot her."*

Under questioning from the Prosecution Hubert said that he was amazed when his mother told him to shoot and the next thing he remembered was seeing blood on his father's face and his mother screaming. After the shootings he went into his own bedroom and put some clothes into a suitcase. He denied going through his father's pockets for money, but did admit taking about £100 and heading for London.

The tragedy of the case could not have been more poignant. The jury had what seemed a simple verdict to deliver. Hubert had confessed to murdering both parents, but could a young lad so deprived of education and so backward in the ways of the world be held entirely responsible for his actions. In the end they had little choice. Hubert was found GUILTY of murdering his father, but strangely not that of murdering his mother. The charge concerning his mother would remain on court files as undecided. Hubert himself was sent to prison where he was to be detained at Her Majesty's Pleasure. The actual length of sentence would be reviewed some time later depending on his progress.

BOYS WILL BE BOYS
Cannock - Leacroft - Hednesford

What is it that makes young lads rush to the back seat on a bus or crave after being the first to be covered in dirt? Why do they hanker after toys or games that have an underlying element of danger or violence? Why are they so ready to use their fists to settle any dispute no matter how trivial? The answer probably lies in their misguided view of what actually makes a man and that no doubt stems from the Victorian attitude, instilled in boys even today, that "men, and that includes boys, don't cry"; they are forced to be "manly", whatever that means. Unfortunately such ideas have led boys to put themselves in danger when common sense would have insisted they avoid it. The following sad stories illustrate just that.

Saturday afternoon on June 19th, 1897 saw a group of lads playing in the playground of the Cannock Workhouse between four and five o'clock when suddenly a fight broke out between two of the lads. Nothing unusual you might think, an everyday occurrence between young lads, but it was to turn tragic. Thomas Hall, aged eleven, struck out at William Cox, aged twelve, and in defence William retaliated. A fight ensued and the next blow from William caught Thomas on the chest. The blow

28. Cannock Workhouse c.1920.

was barely strong enough to do any damage, but Thomas fell to his knees and then down on to his face on to the hard surface. Miss Jellyman, an industrial trainer at the workhouse, was looking out of her window which overlooked the playground and saw the boy lying there. From the crowd of boys who had gathered round she guessed that something untoward was happening and so rushed to the scene. Some lads had already been coming to fetch her.

When she arrived at the scene she realised that poor Thomas was already in a *"dying condition"* and after placing him in a more comfortable position she ran for help. Mrs. Bullock, the ward woman, came and immediately raised the lad up. Miss Jellyman then went for the nurse, Miss West, and then to get Mr. J.W. Roach, the clerk to the Guardians. Unfortunately all efforts to revive William were unsuccessful.

* *From the description of how the two women treated the body it is difficult to know whether they actually helped the lad or if fact hindered his breathing. We are told today to place the body in the "recovery position" so that the air flow to the lungs is not affected and certainly not to raise the patient up. But remember Victorian nursing ideas were not as advanced as ours are today.*

Dr. Riley, medical officer to the Union, was sent for, but was unavailable at the time. However, he did arrive soon after hearing of the affair, but was unable to make any difference. Thomas's body was taken to Cannock Mortuary (adjacent to Church Street) to await the inquiry which would follow.

* *Thomas Hall came from Norton Canes and even though both his father and mother were still living he had been placed in the workhouse. Due to poverty the father was also in the same institution at the time. As for William Cox he was from Cannock and was an orphan. Both boys had been in the workhouse for some time.*

On Monday June 21st Sergeant Burgess arrested young William Cox and he was taken before the magistrates, Messrs. Bumsted and Evans, at Cannock Petty Sessions and was charged with causing the death of Thomas Hall. The sergeant told the hearing that he was only proposing to outline those preliminary investigations which had already taken place. He said that on being informed of the tragic event he had gone to the workhouse on the Saturday afternoon and had viewed the body of Thomas Hall. He had examined it and found a slight abrasion on the skin on the right temple. He also saw the prisoner and asked him what had happened. The lad said, *"We were playing in the playground. Hall struck me first on the nose and we then fought. As he was coming at me I struck him just here (pointing to the left side of the chest) with my fist. He fell down and never spoke again."* The sergeant then told the court that he would be interviewing further witnesses later.

He then told the hearing that at first the police had thought it best that the prisoner be returned to the workhouse rather than be in custody, but after consultation the Deputy Chief Constable, Captain Longdon, had suggested that he be kept in custody and not delegate the responsibility to those people at the workhouse or anyone else. The Bench agreed and young William Cox was remanded in custody until the following week.

William did not have to wait that long because Mr. W. Morgan, the coroner, opened the inquest on the Monday afternoon with Mr. John Stokes acting as foreman to the jury. Sergeant Burgess represented the police and told the hearing that William Cox was present and in his charge.

The first witness was Annie Jellyman who stated that she had identified the body of the deceased as that of Thomas Hall and that he was eleven years old. She said that on Saturday afternoon she was in her sitting room which overlooked the playground when she saw all the boys near the back door. She ordered them away to the other side. A short while after she saw a boy lying on his side and she went out and asked, *"What is the matter?"* Someone said, *"It's Tommy Hall. He's in a fit."* She then went to him and turned him over and took his arms from under him. He was gasping for breath and so she went for assistance. She was only away a minute or two, but when she returned the lad was dead. He was taken to the mortuary and the doctor was sent for.

She added that one side of the lad's face was covered with blood. The playground was asphalted. When questioned by a juror she said that Thomas was not subject to fits and enjoyed good health.

Thomas Emberton, aged twelve, who had been at the workhouse for one year one month said that on the Saturday afternoon at about 4.30 p.m. all the boys, seventeen of them, were playing in the playground. The deceased said that he would fight William Cox and then he struck Cox on the nose. Cox struck him back, but missed him on the right side. However, he followed it up with a left hand blow which caught Hall on the left side of his chest. Hall struck back again and then Cox struck Hall on the temple. At that the deceased said, *"All right,"* and placed himself in a fighting attitude, but then fell with his face hitting the asphalt. Miss Jellyman came as soon as the lad dropped. As far as he knew the two had had no quarrel previously.

John Man, another eleven year old inmate, said that he was also in the yard at 4.30 p.m. The deceased and Cox were grumbling about something, but he did not know about what. Hall pulled his jacket off and said, *"Come on now,"* and struck first hitting Cox on the nose. Cox retaliated with his right hand but missed. He then followed with a left hand blow to Hall's chest. Hall struck again, but missed and then Cox got Hall's head under his arm and struck him on the head. At that point Hall fell to his knees, shivered a bit and then fell on to his face.

When questioned by the jury Man said that they both had their jackets off and the fight lasted about two and a half minutes; *"It was just an ordinary boys' fight."*

Dr. Riley, medical officer to the Cannock Union, stated that he had never had to attend the deceased for ill-health. On the Saturday he was sent for he was out, but arrived at the workhouse at 6 o'clock and found the lad dead in the mortuary. He had since made a post mortem examination. Externally there was an abrasion on the right side of the face, but nothing serious. Internally all the organs were healthy and generally the lad was fairly well nourished. As far as he was concerned the cause of death was syncope caused by a shock to the nervous system. That might have been caused by a blow and tallied with the evidence given by the previous two witnesses. The injury to the face was trivial and was caused by the deceased falling on to the asphalt. Under questioning Dr. Riley said that he had "no doubt that death was caused by the blow".

The coroner, in summing up, said he was afraid that there was no other conclusion to arrive at given the evidence but that the blow delivered by William Cox caused the death of Thomas Hall. The boys were fighting and that was an "illegal act" and, according to the law of England as it stood then, he was afraid the jury had no other option to adopt but return a verdict of manslaughter.

Mr. Playfer, one of the jury, asked if the lad's age would make any difference. The coroner said that it would not, but it would be taken into consideration before another court (meaning the Assizes). Then several of the jurors asked if it might not be possible for them to return a verdict of accidental death, but Mr. Morgan replied that if persons were committing an illegal act when the death of one occurred it was manslaughter. Again the jury tried to avoid their verdict and another asked if they might return a verdict of misadventure. Once again the coroner repeated his advice and so finally the jury, after a short consultation, returned the verdict of manslaughter.

Mr. Morgan then formally committed William Cox to be tried at the July Assizes at Stafford. Dr. Riley and Mr. Roach said that they were willing to act as sureties for the prisoner until the trial and so Mr. Morgan fixed the bail at £15 each which was entered into.

On July 23rd young William Cox was brought before Lord Chief Justice Russell for the manslaughter of Thomas Hall on June 19th 1987. Mr. C.L. Fisher for the Prosecution said that after examining all the facts of the case he would offer no evidence against the lad. The judge, therefore, DISCHARGED Cox. He was free to return to the Cannock Workhouse, but whether he did or not is not clear. As an orphan he was a ward of the Parish of Cannock and their responsibility, but they might have seen fit to transfer him to another institution.

Barely three months later Cannock was to witness another child fatality. Alfred Brookes, aged four who lived with his grandparents on the canal side at Rumer Hill, was shot in the head while out walking with friends in a lane at Leacroft on the afternoon of Friday, August 27th 1897. Rumour began to swiftly circulate around Cannock that he had been killed by someone shooting in the neighbouring fields. Colour was given to the rumour by young John Foster, aged thirteen, who said that he had been shooting in the road close to where the accident happened when he heard a shot and saw smoke, but he did not know who had fired the shot. A few hours later, however, due to the diligence of the local police, the same lad was arrested on suspicion of being involved in the affair.

It seemed that the police had found out that some three hours before the shooting young John Foster had been seen by another lad in possession of a revolver and some ball cartridges. Police Constable Weaver was sent to question Foster, who at first denied having the revolver. Ultimately he admitted to it and said that he had found it in a field of turnips which belonged to Mr. Devey and had put it back there. That field was subsequently searched, but no revolver was found. Foster was then arrested and later on, in the presence of his father who urged him to tell the truth, he said that he had thrown it into a pit near the popular tree at Leacroft.

Sergeant Burgess and another officer, together with the lad's father, on Saturday morning, set to emptying the pit in question and when they had finished the revolver was found by Constable Weaver in the mud. On the Saturday morning young John Foster was brought before Mr. F.D. Bumsted at Mr. Gardener's office and was then remanded until the following Monday.

Unfortunately little Alfred Brookes had died at about 10.30 p.m. on the Friday night. He had been shot just over the right eye and the bullet had penetrated the brain and lodged at the back of the skull. After he had been shot he had been picked up by Foster who tied a handkerchief around the lad's head and carried him home. He was unconscious all the time and never recovered consciousness before he expired.

The inquest into the sad affair was held at the Railway Hotel, Cannock and began on Monday afternoon, August 30th before Mr. W. Morgan, the coroner, with Mr. Anderson acting as foreman for the jury. There was quite a gathering, all curious to catch a glimpse of young Foster who was led into the room by the police. Once the jury had viewed the body they returned to the court and the first witness was called.

Margaret Brookes, grandmother of the deceased, stated that she was married to William Brookes, a miner, and they lived at Rumer Hill. They had always looked after the lad, Alfred, who was illegitimate, as their daughter was in service in Birmingham. On the Friday afternoon he had left their home at about 4.00 p.m. with their daughter, Alice, aged eight, and Maude Foster who was about four. Some time later at about 4.30 p.m. she was near her house when Ann Smith, a neighbour, called over to her and said, *"Oh Margaret, it's Fred!"* Mrs. Smith then carried Alfred into the house and simply said, *"He's shot."* Margaret asked her who had done it, but Mrs. Smith said that she did not know.

Dr. T.W. Madge came and attended to the lad. She noticed that the lad had a wound over his right eye and a bruise on the left side of his head. Little Alfred never spoke again and died at about 10.25 p.m. the same night.

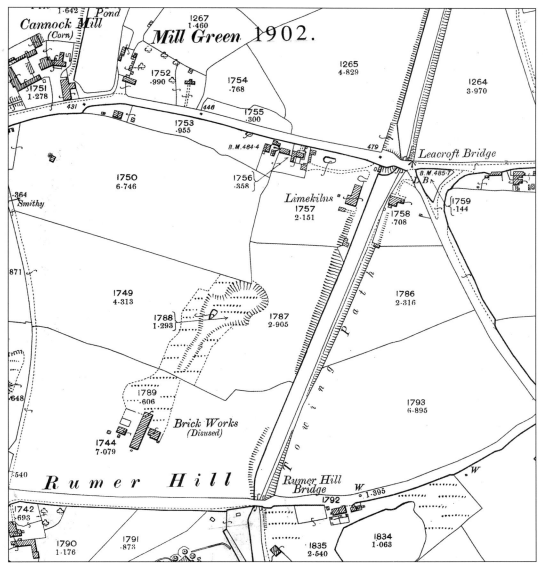

29. Map of Mill Green, Cannock (1902).

The next witness was Edward Richard Doughty of Cannock, aged sixteen, who was employed by Mr. John Sellman of Hall Court as a stableman. He stated that at about 1.00 p.m. on the Friday he went to the Cannock Mill to fetch some chaff. The prisoner, John Foster, was employed at the Mill and came over to help the witness load his cart. The witness pulled off his jacket and put it in the chaff house. That jacket had a revolver in the left hand pocket and two cartridges in the right one. At about 2.30 p.m. the same day he realised that the revolver and cartridges were missing. He next saw them in the possession of the police on the Sunday.

When questioned about carrying a gun at his young age Doughty said that his master had given it to him for his safety while going errands and doing other work.

However, he was carrying it that day because he was trying to sell it.

Eight year old Alice Brookes was next to give evidence. She said that on the Friday afternoon she was going up the road at Leacroft by Mr. Dean's field with Maud Foster and Alfred Brookes when John Foster overtook them. He asked his sister to go with him and they went up the road in front of Alice and her brother. John Foster then turned round and looked towards them. It was then that she heard what she thought was a gun go off in Mr. Bird's field. As soon as the shot was fired her brother fell down in the road. She looked towards Maud and John Foster, but could not see them for smoke. When that cleared John got over the hedge into Mr. Dean's field and then came back into the road the same way.

John was walking up the road when she asked him to pick Freddy up. He did so and then asked, *"Who's got a handkerchief?"* She gave him hers and John tied it round her brother's head and then carried him off down the road. As they were going down the road they met Mrs. Smith who took her brother into the house.

John Chadbend, aged ten, from Old Penkridge Road said that at about 4.15 p.m. on the Friday he was in the road at Leacroft when he saw all four there. They were about twelve yards in front of him near the popular tree. He suddenly heard the sound of a gun and saw Alfred Brookes fall down. He also witnessed some smoke where the other children were standing. After the shot John Foster got over the hedge into a field on the left hand side going from Cannock. The prisoner appeared to look over the fence into the next field where there was a pit. He then came back into the road and the witness asked him what was the matter. Foster said that someone had shot Alfred in the right side of the head. Foster then picked the lad up and asked for a handkerchief. The witness also heard Foster say to the deceased, *"Freddy, stand up."* After the lad was carried away the witness continued up the road towards Leacroft Colliery.

John Edward Joseph, aged ten of Walsall Road, said that at 1.40 p.m. he was at Mill Green, Cannock when he met the prisoner who had a revolver in his hand. While he was with the prisoner Foster pushed an empty cartridge out of the barrel with a steel rod. He then showed the witness a cartridge which had not been fired. Foster held the revolver while the witness examined it. At that point the witness was shown the revolver and he was sure it was the same one that Foster showed him. He was then questioned about the possible conversation he had with the prisoner, but could offer no evidence which would have had an importance to the hearing.

Sergeant Burgess told the hearing that John Foster was arrested by Constable Weaver on the Friday evening and brought to the Cannock Police Station and charged with unlawfully wounding Alfred Brookes. The boy made a statement and was then locked up. The following morning Mr. Foster arrived at the station and the lad was brought from the cells. Mr. Foster said to his son, *"Now, John, if you have done this, tell the truth about it. Tell them where the pistol is."* The prisoner then replied, *"I told*

Mr. Weaver last night where it is. It is in the turnip field where I found it. I took it back and put it there."

Sergeant Burgess then told the hearing that he then said, *"Oh, that place has been searched and the gun is not there at all."* On hearing that Mr. Foster said, *"Tell us the truth about it,"* and the prisoner said, *"Well, I threw it in the old pool near the popular tree. You know where I mean. You will find it there close to the side."* The witness then went with the prisoner, Mr. Foster and Constable Weaver to the pool and the constable found the gun in the mud. He handed it to the witness who examined it and discovered two empty cartridges in it.

Constable Weaver stated that from information received he went to the prisoner on the Friday evening and asked him where the pistol was that he had had at dinner time. The prisoner replied that he had never had one. The witness then asked him to tell the truth and the prisoner replied, *"I did find one in the bottom of Mr. Devey's turnip field."* When asked where it was now the lad said that he had put it back where he had found it. When asked to show the witness exactly where it was the lad accompanied him to the field and pointed out a spot where it was. It was nowhere to be found and so he told the lad that he was not satisfied that he was being told the truth. He then took him to Cannock Police Station.

Once there and in front of Sergeant Burgess the witness told the lad that he did not think he was telling the truth. It was then that the prisoner said, *"I was in the road at Leacroft and had a pistol. I was with Maud Foster and Alice and Alfred Brookes. I pulled the trigger and it went off and struck Alfred on the left side of the head. I don't know what was in it. I did not load it."* It was at that point that John Foster was charged.

The constable also told the hearing that previous to the statement in the station the prisoner had told him that he had heard the shot, seen the smoke, but had not known who had fired the gun.

Dr. Madge, acting as locum for the absent Dr. Butter, said that he went to see Alfred Brookes at about five o'clock. He found the lad in bed suffering from a bullet wound over the right brow. There were no marks of burning powder. The lad was unconscious and never regained consciousness. It was a "hopeless case" from the start. He went again at ten o'clock and found the lad rapidly sinking. He had since made a

30. Police on duty in Brunswick Road.

post mortem examination and found the bullet in the back of the cerebellum. The bullet had passed through the brain and had partially flattened itself against the skull. The bullet wound causing great haemorrhage was undoubtedly the cause of death. Because of the lack of powder burns he thought the shot was fired three to four feet from the deceased, but still close.

At that point in the hearing John Foster was asked if he had anything to say, but said that he had not. He was obviously very shaken and on sitting down he fainted and was taken from the room.

The coroner in summing up said that there was no doubt that Alfred Brookes had been killed by John Foster, but the jury had to decide one of three possibilities – was it a case of wilful murder; or that there was such culpable negligence on the part of John Foster as would amount to manslaughter; or was it death by misadventure. As for the first scenario there was no evidence of malice aforethought and so that could be dismissed. As to the suggestion of manslaughter the coroner pointed out that there had been two cartridges in the gun, one of which Foster had obviously fired beforehand. He therefore must have known the power of the revolver and so pointing it at another person and firing it he should have known its consequences.

The jury retired and after a ten minute discussion returned a verdict of Death from Misadventure. They also expressed a wish that the legislature on the carrying of firearms should be tightened. Also they recommended that the lad Doughty should be reprimanded because he had not shown sufficient care of the weapon. Fortunately for him he was not in court at the time and escaped the coroner's wrath.

After the inquest John Foster was taken to Hednesford to appear before Mr. Wolverton J.P where he was charged with causing Alfred Brookes' death and remanded until the following Monday, bail being fixed at £10 and on surety of £10.

Although an inquest jury may find a person not guilty of the serious crime of murder or manslaughter as in this case the coroner does not have the legal power to discharge the person. That can only be granted by a magistrate or judge. Mr. Wolverton obviously thought there was a serious case to answer.

On Monday September 6th John Foster appeared before the magistrates at Cannock and after reviewing the evidence he was sentenced to be tried at the coming Stafford Assizes. He was then charged with stealing a revolver, valued at 7s 6d, from Edward Richard Doughty. Of that crime he was found guilty and sentenced to receive six strokes of the birch.

On December 2nd, 1897 at the Stafford Assizes before Judge Justice Lawrence the jury found a true bill against John Foster who pleaded guilty. Justice Lawrence, after a short consultation with Mr. Foster, and after addressing the lad said that, although he was the cause of the death of Alfred Brookes, he thought it "little more than an accident". He, therefore, hoped Foster *would make it his duty to keep up the good character that had been given of him and that his present position would be a warning to him".* He therefore DISCHARGED young John Foster with Mr. Foster becoming surety of £10 as to his son's future behaviour.

The final case in this tragic chapter follows the same pattern as the previous one and happened in 1945. The main difference from the Victorian cases above was that the local newspaper, *The Cannock Advertiser,* decided not to publish the name of the young perpetrator as he was under sixteen. However, they did publish the victim's name and so it would be quite easy for prying gossips at the time to work out exactly who the perpetrator might have been. I have decided to keep the anonymity of both, merely referring to them as X and Y. The same will apply to their respective families.

On Tuesday night on January 16th 1945 both lads were at the Hednesford Drill Hall attending a training course as members of the Army Cadet Force 2nd Battalion, E Company, Staffordshire. At nine o'clock the parade had been dismissed and a group of the lads were in the vestibule about to leave. Suddenly a shot rang out and boy X fell to the floor quite dead. The police were immediately called and Inspector Brown of Hednesford arrived at 9.30 p.m. and having been told what had happened arrested boy Y and took him to Hednesford Police Station. The victim's body was removed to the mortuary at Hednesford (along Victoria Street, opposite the park).

On the Wednesday the lad, dressed in his cadet uniform, appeared before the Juvenile Court at Cannock and was charged with manslaughter, by law the only charge that could be given until further investigations had taken place. After the evidence of arrest had been given the hearing was adjourned until January 31st by which time the inquest would have taken place. The boy Y had made a statement, but it was decided not to put that to the hearing at that time. The Chairman of the Court, Alderman A. Whitehouse, said that he understood that the shooting "was in the nature of an accident" and he turned and said to Y, *"Look after yourself and don't let this*

31. The Drill Hall, Hednesford c.1940.

matter over worry you." Sound advice we might think, but Y was clearly terrified and upset.

Although the Press did not name the lad reporters still had their job to do and so they interviewed anyone they thought might be able to give them information. Captain J.G. Stevenson, OC of the Company, said that the incident had nothing to do with the training and that the weapon had nothing at all to do with the company or its training. He also stated that the victim was a *very good lad, tremendously keen on his training"* and he was to have sat for an examination on the Saturday with all the other lads.

Callously they also interviewed X's father and mother of Booth Street, Hednesford who told them that it was *"a terrible shock to the family when the news was broken to them that evening"*. Their son had left home at 7.00 p.m. to go to training. He was desperately keen on the Army Cadet Force and attended every parade and had done so since the August. He was educated at West Hill Boys School and later went to Littleworth Senior School. When he left there he had first worked at Hednesford Wagon Repairs on Cannock Road, but had left there and gone to work at Messrs. H. Hawkins at Bridgtown. He would have been sixteen in the May.

The inquest before Mr. W.M. Morgan, son of the coroner in the previous two cases, was held on Friday January 19th at Hednesford. The police report stated that on Tuesday evening, January 15th three lads were at the Drill Hall after the cadet parade had dismissed. They were in the entrance hall when the accused produced a revolver. The boy X said, *"Fire it"* and the accused lad, standing about four feet away and holding the revolver in his right hand, pulled the trigger. It went off and the lad X immediately fell to the floor quite dead. The police were sent for and having interviewed the accused they arrested him. Inspector Brown said that later a bullet was discovered in the entrance hall. When the coroner commented, *"I take it that, mercifully, death would have been instantaneous"*, the Inspector agreed.

Dr. G.M. Torrance, police surgeon, said that he had arrived at the Drill Hall at 9.20 p.m. and found the victim already dead. He later conducted a post mortem and found a wound half an inch in diameter on the left side of the nose. The bullet had gone through the brain and out through the back of the head. The wound was consistent with the firing of the revolver being at close range.

The only other witness at the inquest was X's father who told the hearing that his son knew nothing about revolvers as far as he knew. He did know about air guns. He also told the hearing that his son and Y were *"big friends and on particularly good terms"*. They worked at the same place and went to the parades together. He and his wife were also friendly with Y's parents.

In his summing up Mr. Morgan said to the jury, *"I am sure it would be your first wish to join with me in expressing sympathy with the relatives in this most unfortunate and tragic occurrence. We do indeed sympathise most deeply with the father, more so when his boy was engaging on duties which are uppermost in many boys' minds these days. His son had joined this splendid movement and it is indeed a tragedy that he should have met his death in this way."* He then closed the inquest SINE DIE (indefinitely).

Although the coroner's judgement was that there were no further facts to be learned that could alter his decision the case still had to go before the court and so on Wednesday January 30th the lad once more stood before the Juvenile Court at Cannock. Before the case was heard Mr. William Henry Evans, a married man who lodged at George Street, Hednesford, was charged with being in possession of a firearm without having a certificate. Mr. Cooper, prosecuting, said that Evans had acquired it whilst serving in enemy territory during the war. He had no right to keep it without a certificate, but there was no suggestion that the lack of a certificate had anything to do with the tragedy.

Inspector Brown said that he had interviewed Evans who had made a statement to the affect that he had served with the forces in France and was later transferred to the reserve to take up a civilian job. He had got the pistol during the evacuation of Dunkirk and kept it as a souvenir. He had shown the revolver to the defendant and told him all about it. As far as he knew the lad had never fired it and had never been given permission to take it. In reply to a question from the chairman, Alderman J. Baker, Evans said that he had not inquired as to whether he needed a certificate or not. Realising his mistake and his inadvertent part in the tragedy Evans pleaded guilty and was fined 40 shillings with £1 1s costs.

When the actual case started Mr. Cooper outlined the tragic events of the Tuesday evening. He said that the defendant had taken the pistol without permission to the Drill Hall that night to show his friends, possibly to "appear big with his pals". He also took two magazines, one empty, but the other contained two cartridges. The parade started at 7.30 p.m. and finished at about 9.00 p.m. When they were dismissed three lads, X, Y and another lad were in the entrance hall. The third lad noticed something bulky in the accused's pocket and asked to see it. Y then produced the pistol. When X approached to see it the accused had apparently put the magazine containing the two cartridges into the gun. X then said, *"Fire"* and the accused pointed it at him and pulled the trigger. X was shot through the head and died instantly.

The other lad, named Jones, described to the court what had happened. He said that he had asked Y what was in his pocket and Y had produced the gun. X had said, *"Fire"* and there was a bang. The accused appeared to be startled when X fell to the floor.

Second Lieutenant William Arthur Beckett of Mount Side Street, Hednesford stated that he was in charge of the parade that night and he was in the orderly room when he heard a shot. He rushed to the entrance hall and saw X in a collapsed condition, being supported by the accused and another lad. He heard someone say that X had been shot with a 22 and the accused handed him the pistol and said, *"This is what I done it with."* He later searched the entrance and found a bullet near to where X had been standing. He later gave it to the police.

Police Constable Tomson who stayed with the accused at Hednesford Police Station said that the accused said, *"I shot him, sir. I didn't know the revolver was working."* He then advised the lad to say nothing more. The lad was crying and was very distressed. He also told the court that he had been unable to trace the spent cartridge or the second cartridge on the fatal evening.

Inspector Brown said that the lad made a statement whilst at the police station. It stated that X had said *"Fire"* or something like that. He thought he was pointing at something in the air. *"The revolver went off. I did not think it would. I saw X on the floor and thought he was playing."* He said that he had no idea the gun would go off because he had previously pulled the trigger on a number of occasions without anything happening. He added that when he picked X up he saw that he was bleeding. He went out to get a doctor, but someone else had gone and so he returned to the hall and knelt by X. He had borrowed the revolver several times before.

Mr. Cooper for the Prosecution then addressed the Bench and said that the accused had no right to have the pistol. However, no malice or intent was suggested; that would be murder. The two lads were particularly good friends, but the fact remained that Y pulled the trigger and killed X. In his opinion that was manslaughter. The Bench did not have to decide the punishment as that would be a matter for a higher court, but did have to decide whether a case had been made out for the defendant to go for trial. He thought that the Bench would be convinced that the pistol went off accidentally, but even so it would still be their duty to say that a case had to be answered.

The Bench agreed and Y was committed for trial at the next Assizes on the charge of manslaughter. Mr. Haden for the Defence applied for bail and legal aid, both of which were granted.

In March, 1945 Y appeared before Mr. Justice Wrottesley at the Stafford Quarter Sessions. All the evidence heard the jury found Y guilty of causing the accidental death of X. The judge turned to Y and said, *"By carelessness you killed a boy, who they tell me, was your best friend. Such carelessness is often very severely punished, but you have a very good character and we don't expect to find old heads on young shoulders always."* He therefore BOUND Y OVER FOR TWELVE MONTHS as he felt that was the most appropriate sentence.

Historical Note - The idea of a volunteer force first came into being in 1859 because of the possible threat from France. Most of our regular troops were out in India dealing with the aftermath of the Indian Mutiny of 1857 and so the Volunteers were formed to safeguard England. A number of the volunteers groups formed Cadet Companies of young lads. By 1908 the title Cadet Force was introduced and the Territorial Army Association took over the administration of the Cadet Force. With World War One in 1914 the Cadet Force greatly expanded and the War Office took over its administration. In 1942 the title Army Cadet Force was introduced.

Hednesford's volunteer force was set up in 1892 by Captain Williamson as Company F of the Staffordshire Volunteer Force and in 1894 the Drill Hall was opened as a base for training. 1914 saw them in action when Captain William Burnett led his men off to fight in the trenches. Sometime in the late 1960's they moved from the Drill Hall to a purpose built hall next door. Today they meet in a brand new building just inside Hednesford Park.

WHEN LIFE'S TOO MUCH
Norton Canes and Wimblebury

Depression is that strange illness which is so difficult to define and even more difficult to cope with when it strikes. It causes can be many – money difficulties, loss of one's job and seemingly no prospects of another, lack of love in one's life or even sexual frustration. Whatever the reasons there seem to be common outcomes – a feeling of unworthiness and lack of self-confidence. Daily tasks become a drudge and to some sufferers, a nightmare. It can be at that point when the desperate seek the most desperate solution. Unfortunately the law, though possibly sympathetic to the plight of the victim of depression, has to take its course as the following tragic cases will testify.

On Friday 19th July, 1907 James Middleton was sitting on the towpath of the canal at Norton Canes fishing when a woman came towards him with a young child at her side. He asked her the time and after she had told him she moved on. Not much further along she suddenly grabbed the child and jumped into the canal. Without thinking James rescued her and the child and then sought out help. As attempted suicide and murder of the child was obviously a crime the police soon became involved and the woman was arrested.

At the Cannock Police Court on Monday, July 22nd Ethel Nellie Bladon, aged 26, *"a frail, delicate looking little woman"* was charged with attempted murder and suicide. Police Constable Adams stated that she had gone to the station voluntarily and whilst there had told him that she had been unwell lately and had not been able to do her work for some time. She did not want to be a trouble to her master and mistress as they had been kind to her and if her husband, who had left her, had sent money towards the maintenance of the boy she would never have tried to do what she did.

At that stage the case was adjourned until the Wednesday morning when further evidence would be forthcoming. On the Wednesday at the Special Court held at the Public Rooms, Cannock before Mr. F.D. Bumsted she was again charged with the attempted murder of her son, William, and the attempted suicide. Because she was so frail she was supplied with a chair and watched the whole proceedings "in an apathetic manner".

James Middleton, a labourer from Stafford Street, Heath Hayes, said that he was on the Birmingham Canal towpath in Norton Canes at about 8.30 p.m. fishing when he saw the prisoner carrying a child along the path in the direction of the Fair Lady Wharf. She did not see him until she was quite close as he was sitting in the grass. He then asked her the time and she replied that it was 8.30 p.m. He saw her go along the canal a further 150 yards and then she approached the side of the water and suddenly jumped in with the child in her arms. He ran along and jumped in after her. She came to the surface and when she saw him close by she said, *"Don't fetch me out, let me die."* Despite that he caught hold of one of her arms – she had the child in the other – and he got her to the side which was bricked.

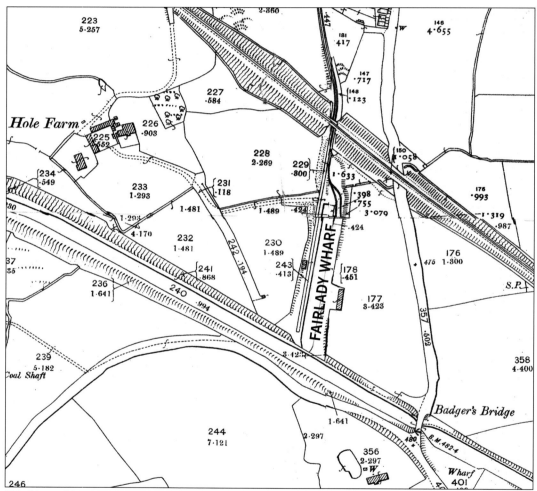

32. Map of Norton Canal (1902).

He got out himself and then caught hold of her under her arms and dragged her out with the child. After that he asked her what she had done it for and she replied that it was all through her husband who had left her. He asked her who he was and she replied, *"Alfred Bladon,"* whom the witness knew very well. He then asked her where she was living and she said, *"Mr. Fellows."* He then asked her if she would go home without him going with her to which she replied, *"No. I shall do it again if I get the chance. You ought to have let me and the child die."* Because of that he took the child from her and escorted her to the house of Constable Adams. Unfortunately the constable was not in and so he said that he would take her to Mr. Fellows. When they reached Beadle's house the witness asked where the child lived and the prisoner said, *"Here,"* (meaning Beadle's). The prisoner took the child into Mrs. Beadle and he went and fetched Miss Fellows.

* John Beadle, aged 61, lived with his wife, Clara aged 60, in Norton Village. He was a coal miner/fireman and the pair had raised a family of four children, three sons and a daughter, who had by then left home. To make ends meet they took in children to look after.

When Miss Fellows arrived she asked the prisoner why she had tried to kill herself and the child and the prisoner replied, *"To end all my troubles."* At that point she began to cry. The witness then left and at about 9.45 p.m. he met Constable Adams and told him what had happened.

Miss Emily Fellows said that she lived at Norton Canes in Norton Village with her brother, Mr. John Fellows, and the prisoner, Ethel Nellie Bladon, had been their domestic servant for some years before her marriage. (John Fellows was a colliery and estate agent and the vice chairman of the Cannock Board of Guardians at the time.) Ethel's husband had deserted her and the child some three and a half years ago and so they took her back into service again. At about 7.00 p.m. on the Friday evening she had left Ethel at her duties and some time after eight o'clock, because

The Canal, Norton.

33. Norton Canal c.1940.

of something she had been told, the witness went to the house of John Beadle and saw the prisoner there with the child. They were both very wet, but did not show any signs of exhaustion.

The witness then said that she had asked Ethel why she had tried to kill herself and the child and her reply was, *"To get out of my troubles."* She had also said that her head was bad and that she could not do her work. When questioned Miss Fellows said that she had noticed that the prisoner had looked pale a few days previously, but she had attributed that to the hot weather. The prisoner had done her work as usual and there was nothing in her behaviour to lead the witness to believe anything was wrong.

Miss Fellows then told the court that prior to the accused making an attempt on her own life and that of her child she had sent the witness a letter which contained a photograph of little William and a cutting from a newspaper in which her husband had given notice that he would not be responsible for any debts incurred by his wife - the proverbial nail in the coffin?

The next witness was Richard Alex S. Eden, a medical practitioner at Norton Canes. He stated that when he first saw the prisoner she "appeared to be in a weak and nervous state" and complained of pain in the head. He gave her directions as to her treatment and visited her again in the afternoon. She then said that she felt much better and wanted to get up. He then certified her for removal to the Workhouse Infirmary at Cannock. When he saw her on the Saturday morning after the incident he asked her how it had happened and she replied, *"I did it on purpose."*

When questioned Mr. Eden said that the prisoner had been under his treatment several times during the last year suffering from neuralgic pains, anaemia and weakness. (Unfortunately in those early days doctors knew very little about depression and even less on how to treat it. Some even believed it was madness. At least Mr. Eden recommended the infirmary for a rest and not the local "madhouse".)

The final witness was Constable Adams who repeated his previous evidence and

34. Constable Smith of Norton Canes.

added that about Christmas last the accused had spoken to him about her husband and had asked him to try and find him. He had made inquiries for her, but unfortunately could not discover his whereabouts.

With all the witnesses heard Mr. Bumsted asked Ethel if she desired bail, but she declined it. He then said that he thought *"the rest would do her good"*, but it was his duty to formally commit her for trial at the forthcoming Assizes.

It was on Tuesday, 12th November 1907 when Ethel Bladon stood before Mr. Justice Jelf at the Stafford Assizes. Mr. Bosanquet for the Prosecution began by saying that on the advice of Judge Mr. Milward the defendant had changed her plea from not guilty to guilty. He then outlined the sad events of the case detailing the unfortunate marriage and the abandonment by her husband. Miss Fellows and her brother had been kind enough to re-employ her and they had paid her 4s 6d per week, together with her board and lodgings. Out of that she had to pay 4s per week to board out her little boy, William, with the Beadle family which only left her 6d per week for her own clothes and those of her child. Her husband had refused to pay anything towards their upkeep.

* In 1901 William "Alfred" Bladon, aged 19, was lodging with John Burdett (26) and his wife, Harriett (24) and young daughter, Florence (4), in Stafford Street, Heath Hayes. He was a coal miner and had met and married Ethel Nellie Talbot, one year his senior, around 1903. She had moved from her position with the Fellows family and set up home with William, but the marriage did not last long. For reasons unknown he had deserted them and Ethel had luckily been re-employed by Emily Fellows as a servant.

Mr. Bosanquet revealed that she had written several letters which she had left behind at Miss Fellow's home before attempting to drown herself and the child. One letter was addressed to her husband in which she complained that he had not sent her sufficient money for the support of the child and went on to say that he was not worthy to be called father. She also said in it that she hoped that he would be haunted until he died for his treatment of them and finished it by saying, *"they will find Willie and me in the water"*. In another letter she wrote that ever since her son had been born she had suffered with her head.

Once the various witnesses had been heard Mr. Cartlidge, Secretary of the Police Court Mission, entered the witness box at the request of the judge. He said that arrangements had been made for the prisoner to go to a situation at once and a relative had undertaken to look after the child. They would each be well looked after and under the observation of the Mission. The judge then told the jury that the prisoner had been driven to commit the act by her desperate situation, but he recommended that she be BOUND OVER and only to come up for judgement if called on. The jury were in total agreement.

On the Wednesday morning Mr. Bosanquet asked leave of the court to mention the bravery of James Middleton who had rescued them from the canal and hoped the judge would recommend him to the Royal Humane Society. The judge fully agreed and also made an order for James to receive a reward of £5 to be paid by the High Sheriff and recovered from the county.

While the case above had a somewhat happy ending the next was anything but that. Herbert John Stokes, a *"simple"* man, had married on February 18th 1929 and he and his wife, Elizabeth, had gone to live with her parents until they could find lodgings. On May 24th 1929 they had a baby boy whom they named John Herbert. Seven months later they found lodgings with Mrs. Morgan at 19 Wimblebury Road, Heath Hayes. Unfortunately for the couple Herbert was a very jealous man and, without any reason, began to suspect Mr. Morgan of having designs on Elizabeth. It got so bad that Mr. Morgan asked them to leave. They left and found other lodgings in Wimblebury. However, that did not alter Herbert's behaviour and on June 16th 1930 they were again asked to leave and find new lodgings.

The same day they went in search of somewhere to live, but could find nothing. The following day Herbert went on his own and returned to tell Elizabeth that he had found new lodgings. Tired of his behaviour Elizabeth told him that instead of going to the new place she was going back to her mother's and taking little John Herbert with her. On hearing that Herbert snatched the child and ran from the house shouting that he was going to kill both himself and the child. He then raced off to a pool nearby and jumped in. Elizabeth followed, screaming as she went, which alerted men close by. Somehow they managed to drag Herbert from the water, but the child had been drowned already.

Eventually the body was recovered and in the meantime Herbert had been taken to Hednesford Accident Home to recover from his shock. Doctors were called and after they had administered treatment the police were involved. He was arrested for the murder of his son and also charged with attempted suicide. Instead of being held at Cannock Police Station he was transferred to Winson Green Prison, Birmingham where he could undergo medical examination.

On Tuesday June 26th he was brought before Mr. T.A. Hawkins, magistrate, at Cannock Police Court. On Stokes's behalf Mr. Tucker, his Defence lawyer, pleaded not guilty to both charges and reserved his defence. Mr. Ross Pashley acted for the Prosecution and made it clear from the start that he would call Mrs. Stokes as he was allowed under a new law concerning the murder of a child. (Previously wives could not testify against their husbands.)

The first witness was Mrs. Robinson of 35 Glover Street, Wimblebury. She told the court that Mr. and Mrs. Stokes had come to lodge with her on February 10th 1930, occupying the front living room and the back bedroom, and had stayed with her until June 17th. Between nine and ten o'clock on that day she heard Stokes tell his wife that he had got some fresh lodgings and heard Mrs. Stokes say that she was not going to go, but was going home and taking the baby with her. The witness then went into the wash house and about ten minutes later she heard Mrs. Stokes scream in the front room. The witness went as quickly as she could and saw the prisoner running down the road with the baby in his arms and Mrs. Stokes running after him. He was heading towards the pool known locally as the "open pool".

35. 29/37 Glover Street, Wimblebury.

Under questioning Mrs. Robinson said that while they lived with her the prisoner was *"very jealous minded"* and would not allow his wife to go through the door alone. If she had to go out he would watch her. Several times the witness overheard him threaten to *"do his wife and child in"*. As to the child he did not treat him properly and if he cried he would pick him up and strike him. As to work, the witness said he would not go. He had been stopped (sacked) at the Coppice Colliery a fortnight previously. After that he was on the dole for which he got 14s 3d per week which he gave to his wife. On the Monday before the tragedy he had gone out with the intention of going to the Cannock and Rugeley Colliery and East Cannock Colliery to get work, but had found none.

The witness's husband had told them they must find other lodgings as he had caught Stokes watching him over the curtain. For some unknown reason Stokes thought Mr. Robinson had designs on Mrs. Stokes. Her husband had also accused Stokes of listening at the keyhole on occasions. That had caused ill feeling. On the Monday before the tragedy the prisoner had gone to find new lodgings and at that time Mrs. Stokes was apparently willing to go to them. Finally she added that since the war (WWW1) Stokes had been under the doctor. (More would be made of that later.)

Paul Christian Thomas of Arthur Street, Wimblebury said that he was standing near his house overlooking the pool at about 11.00 a.m. Because of shouting he looked towards the pool and saw what he thought was a man in the water. The man had his back towards him and was going further into the water with his arms over his head. The witness fetched a clothes line and went to the pool. When he got there the prisoner seemed to be kneeling. He was under the water in about six or seven feet of water. The rope was put around a man named Caswell who went in and fetched the prisoner out. They revived him on the bank.

John Caswell, a miner of Arthur Street, said that he went down to the pool because of all the noise. Someone then tied a rope around him and he went into the water which was clear. He managed to see a black object in about eight feet of water and about twelve feet from the bank. He went towards the object, discovered it was the prisoner and brought him up. As he was bringing him up his foot touched something *"soft and yielding"* which he thought was the child. He tried to drag it along with him but failed.

36. 40/46 Arthur Street, Wimblebury.

James Stevens, a miner living at 44 Glover Street, Wimblebury, said that at 10.45 a.m. on June 17th he went to the open pool and saw Stokes some twelve or thirteen feet towards the centre of the water. Stokes was got from the water unconscious and a few minutes later the witness put a drag into the water and pulled out the body of the child. That would have been about fifteen to twenty minutes after Stokes was pulled out.

Harold Southall of Tileries Yard, Littleworth said that he saw a man running down the bank with a child in his arms. He saw the man throw the child into the water first and then go in himself. The witness ran back home with his own child and when he got back to the pool Stokes had already been got out. Under questioning he said that he had been on the opposite side of the pool to where the prisoner was and was about fifty or sixty yards away when he first saw him.

Police Constable Bailey said that, after receiving information, he went to the pool and saw Stokes lying on the bank in a very wet condition. He was unconscious but breathing. He was put on to a stretcher and taken to Hednesford Accident Home. The prisoner did not open his eyes while he was there. It was he who gave Stevens a drag and a rope. Having gone a little way towards the Accident Home he was called back by Stevens and the child's body had been recovered. He stayed with the prisoner until about 9 p.m. when he was relieved. Stokes had recovered consciousness at about 3 p.m.

Inspector Dale said that the prisoner was detained at the Accident Home until June 20th. When he arrested him the prisoner said, *"I lost my head. Nothing else."* When he charged him with attempted suicide the prisoner said, *"I did not mean to take my life."* When asked the inspector said that the pool was about 260 yards from where Stokes lodged and it was about 450 feet long and 5 feet deep where Stokes got in.

37. Hednesford Accident Home c.1940.

Dr. J.G. Mitchell of Hednesford said that he arrived at the Accident Home at 11.20 a.m. and saw Stokes brought in. He was extremely ill and his physical condition was very bad. He was suffering from the effects of immersion in water and artificial respiration had been applied previously. He stayed with him a short time and left when he was out of immediate danger. He saw the prisoner twice again that day and on his final visit his condition had much improved. He did not consider at any time that the prisoner's mental condition was abnormal.

Dr. Richard Holton of Hednesford saw the prisoner in bed on June 17th at the Accident Home and again on June 18th. He did not notice anything abnormal in his condition. On June 18th he made a post mortem examination of the child. The child was well nourished and there were no signs of external injury. The cause of death was asphyxia consistent with drowning.

Elizabeth Annie Stokes who elected to give evidence said that she had first met Herbert Stokes about three years ago and after they married they lived with her parents at Hednesford Road, Heath Hayes and stayed there about seven months. They then moved to lodge with Mrs. Morgan and remained there until January 30th 1930 when they moved to 35 Glover Street with Mrs. Robinson. She told the court that from the time they were married her husband was very jealous and could not bear her out of his sight. He used to follow her wherever she went, even if she only went upstairs. He was even jealous of Mr. Robinson, but he had no cause whatsoever. It was that jealousy which forced Mrs. Robinson to ask them to leave.

On the day of the tragedy he told her that he had found new lodgings, but she told him that she did not want to go; instead she would go back to her parents' home. At that he snatched the child, ran to the door and shouted, *"I will drown myself and*

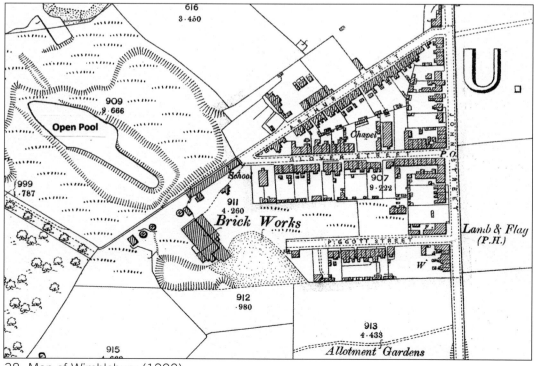

38. Map of Wimblebury (1902).

the child!" He ran down the road very quickly with the child under his arms and she raced after him. When she got to the pool he was in the water stooping with the child between his knees. He was holding the baby head downwards with his hands. All she could do was look on. She was too frightened to go into the water as he had threatened to kill her also beforehand. He had tried to strangle her in the past.

With all the evidence given Mr. Hawkins committed Herbert John Stokes to await trial at the next Assizes. In the meantime he was first taken to Cannock Police Station and then transferred to Winson Green.

Herbert John Stokes did not have long to wait in gaol because his trial began on June 30th 1930 before Mr. Justice McCardie. As at the magistrates' court Mr. Tucker defended Stokes and Mr. Maddocks acted for the Prosecution. During the review of the case Mr. Maddocks referred to the evidence to be given by Mrs. Stokes and that brought the judge to question her viability as a witness. He asked, *"Is the evidence of the wife admissible?* Is she a competent witness at all?"* Mr. Maddocks tried to reassure the judge that she was and quoted precedents in law which allowed the testimony of a wife. That led his lordship to say, *"You can put your case to the jury without referring further to the evidence of the wife and when you have completed your opening I will then adjourn for a time so that you and your learned friend may look into this point together and ascertain the basis on which the wife is a competent witness."* As for the precedents he replied, *"I am here to administer the law and not to allow precedents which may be inaccurate. It may be you are quite right, but I think the point should be considered."* Seems as though his lordship was not quite up to scratch with the new law which seems very strange or did he simply not agree with it?

Mr. Maddocks, having concluded his summing up of the case, told the jury that the Defence would argue that their client was guilty but insane. He stated that to do that they would have to prove that Stokes did not know the nature and gravity of his act or, if he did know what he was doing, that he did not know it was wrong. It was then that the judge adjourned for a while. Considerable argument then followed as to the admissibility of the wife's evidence, but the judge finally agreed that in this particular case it was admissible. Mr. Tucker though asked the judge to warn Mrs. Stokes about their debate when she entered the witness box.

That decided Mr. Maddocks called all the witnesses who had appeared at the previous hearing. Their evidence was the same as before. It was then time to call Elizabeth Stokes. As requested the judge told her that she did not have to give evidence if she so wished but Elizabeth insisted. Having told the court the events of that tragic day she admitted that her marriage had not been a happy one due to her husband's jealousy – he was even jealous of her brothers. He was not kind to their baby knocking *"the child about scandalously".* As for work she said that he would not go.

Mr. Tucker for the Defence suggested, *"You are rather vindictive and bitter towards him, aren't you?"* to which she agreed after some hesitation. He then said, *"And some of the things you have said are not entirely true, are they?"* Elizabeth was shocked and replied, *"They are true. Do you think I should come here and tell a pack of lies?"* Mr. Tucker then turned towards the death of the baby and questioned her love for the child by saying, *"And yet you never stepped into the water, but watched him for a quarter of an hour?"* Elizabeth retorted, *"If I had gone into the water he would have pulled me in. He had threatened to do me and the child many times."* After that encounter Elizabeth left the witness box.

The emphasis of the trial then turned towards Herbert Stokes's possible insanity which was his lawyer's main plan of defence and new witnesses were called to attempt to clarify Stokes's mental health. The first to be called by Mr. Maddocks was Dr. Irwin of Heath Hayes. He stated that he had tended Stokes on various occasions, the last being May 27th, 1930 for gastritis. He said that Stokes seemed to be *"a depressed, reticent sort of man and it was difficult to get him to talk. He could not express himself well and he brooded more than the average man."* Having regard to Stokes's temperament and nature he thought it might very well affect his mental balance. In his opinion Stokes was not up to the ordinary standard and was of low intelligence; the type of man who could more readily lose his mental balance.

Questioned by the judge Dr.Irwin stated that the evidence he had heard about what happened was consistent with someone suffering with melancholia and that might account for the acute jealousy. The judge then added, *"You have heard how this man's great uncle jumped out of a horse and trap and threw himself into the canal. Would that indicate insanity?"* Irwin replied, *"Insanity in the family, but that did not mean everyone was insane."* Mr. Maddocks then asked poignantly, *"When did it first occur to you that this man was insane?"* to which the doctor replied, *"It did not occur to me that he was insane. Insanity is a difficult thing to define. Stokes was not in such a condition as to make him certifiable."*

The next witness was Dr. M.H. Smith of Winson Green Prison who had observed Stokes since his arrival at the prison on June 20th. He had heard from Stokes's mother that her son had had fits until he was fifteen years old. They had stopped, but Dr. Smith said they could return even after such a long period. As to the prisoner he found him in an *"intense depression"* and it was difficult to get him to say anything, *"he simply sat with his head between his hands looking at the ground"*. When he was asked about the tragedy the prisoner said that he could remember nothing about it after taking the child and leaving the house. He could remember nothing about the actual drowning. After a great deal of observation Dr. Smith concluded that the prisoner *"would not know the gravity of that act he did"*.

Mr. Maddocks then asked, *"From the facts put before you do you think he knew what he was doing when he drowned the child?"* Dr. Smith replied, *"I do not think he* did." Mr. Maddocks then asked, *"Would your opinion be altered if it were true that he had previously threatened his wife and ill-treated the child?"* to which the doctor answered, *"I do not think it would make any difference to my opinion."*

With the Prosecution complete Mr. Tucker called Mrs. Stokes, Herbert's mother, for the Defence. She told the court that her son was *"not sharp and not quite the thing"*. He had had fits until the age of fifteen and they had affected him badly. Despite that he had joined the army in 1917 and within a few months he was in France. He became a prisoner of war in Germany and was forced to work in the mines there. Eventually he was ill and had to go into a German hospital. After that *"his peculiarities"* were more marked. He was nervous and trembled if someone crossed him. He was so peculiar that people, especially children, used to shout after him in the street. She had even had to go out and chastise them on occasions. To add further evidence to show his peculiar behaviour his sister said that after the war it was difficult to converse with him and he did not display the normal interest in things around him.

But did Herbert Stokes's unusual behaviour mean that he was insane? Both Prosecution and Defence gave lengthy arguments for and against such a proposal. The judge summed up the case adding, *"Insanity is a strange and terrible thing. It cannot be wiped out of a family (referring to the great uncle who had drowned himself), but was handed down like a hideous poison. It might leave one generation alone and reappear in the next."* It was for the jury to decide. *"If they were satisfied that the prisoner was of sound mind at the time then their verdict must be wilful murder. If on the other hand they believed the prisoner did not know what he was doing at the time then their verdict must be guilty but insane."*

The jury then retired and after some twenty five minutes returned a verdict of GUILTY BUT INSANE. Herbert John Stokes was then ordered to be detained during His Majesty's pleasure in a prison for the mentally insane. There was not a flicker or change of expression on Stokes's face as he heard the judgement.

MAULED TO DEATH
Rugeley

Today we do not think twice about hopping into the car to drive to anywhere in the country. For those without that convenience the public transport system can take us all over England with just a little planning. But what about our ancestors? In early Victorian England the public had a choice between the new invention of the railway, if it came close to where they lived, or the stage coach. There was another mode of transport, much cheaper, but far slower – the canal barges. It was that latter which Robert Collins would be forced to choose for his wife, Christina, in June, 1839.

In 1832 Christina's first husband, Thomas Ingleby, died leaving his young bride (she was only 30 at the time) alone in the world. Fortunately she met and married Robert Collins in 1838 and the two looked for work in Liverpool. Christina was soon successful finding work as a seamstress, but Robert had more difficulty. He eventually decided to move to London and would send for Christina after he had settled. He managed by May, 1839 to send her a guinea to join him, but that would be far too little to travel by coach or train and so she booked passage with Pickford & Co. on one of their canal barges.

It was the custom for the company to employ the captain of the barge, but its crew was left for him to choose. Unfortunately most were rough and ready men, frequently with suspect histories and possibly trying to evade the law in another part of England. Many went by other names to conceal their true identity. Such was the case in this tragic episode. Christina's transport was captained by James Owen, aged 39, and his crew consisted of George Thomas (alias Dobell) aged 27, William Ellis (alias Lambert) and young fourteen year old William Musson.

The journey began on June 15th at 7.30 p.m. from Preston Brook, but Christina was never to see her husband. At around five o'clock on the

39. Site of the Talbot Inn today.

morning of June 17th her body was discovered floating in the canal at Brindley Bank just outside Rugeley. Her corpse was taken to the Talbot Inn, Rugeley to await a post mortem; meanwhile the four crewmen were arrested. What nightmares and degradation Christina had suffered during that dreadful journey would become apparent at the subsequent trail.

Victorian law was usually very quick, but in this case it would take almost a year for the men to be brought to justice. The post mortem was obviously performed within days and its findings suggested Christina might have been raped before she drowned, but that would leave the question of whether she drowned herself or not due to being raped. Evidence of the journey would be vital if a successful case against the men was to be prosecuted. It was the collecting of that evidence which would take the time, although witnesses along the canal were only too willing to come forward. Perhaps the feeling of guilt that they just might have helped Christina more may have played a part.

There were in fact to be two appearances of the men at the Assize Court in Stafford because of the two charges that were brought – one of rape and one of murder. Before either case young William Musson had been freed of both charges due to his age (they did not believe that one so young could be involved in a rape let alone murder) and he was to give evidence against the others.

At the first trial the Prosecution, headed by Mr. Sergeant Ludlow, proceeded with the charge of rape, but after hearing the evidence the judge, Mr. Justice Williams, ruled that there was insufficient evidence to prove the charge and found the men not guilty. However, the Prosecution persuaded him to postpone the case of murder until the next Assizes as a potential new witness had been found.

The second trial began on Monday, March 16th 1840 before Mr. Baron Gurney. James Owen, George Thomas and William Ellis were charged with the wilful murder of Christina Collins. Reporters of the trial said, *"The prisoners were rather rough looking men and their dress and appearance completely indicated the class to which they belonged. They took their places at the bar with some degree of readiness and manifested great composure during the trial."*

Sergeant Ludlow conducted the Prosecution assisted by Mr. Lee while Mr. Godson, assisted by Mr. Yardley, acted for the Defence. Before he called his witnesses Sergeant Ludlow outlined the case in detail finishing by saying to the jury that they only had three possibilities to decide upon – the deceased might have fallen into the canal accidentally; she might have thrown herself in; or she was wilfully thrown in by all or some of the men.

The first to be called was William Brooks, porter for the Pickford Company at Stoke-upon-Trent. Either he did not hear the call or was embarrassed by what he had to tell, but he was late going into the court (a few minutes) which brought a reprimand from the judge to both him and the Counsel. He said that on Sunday

June 16th he saw a woman passenger in one of the boats of which Owen had command. He heard the woman say to Thomas, *"Leave me alone. I will have nothing to say to you."* She then complained to him of the men's behaviour and enquired about a possible transfer to a coach, but none were available. To calm her down and reassure her Mrs. Brooks travelled in the barge for a few miles and the men's behaviour improved.

Hugh Cordwell, a check clerk to the Trent and Mersey Canal Company at Stone, said that he saw the woman at 7.55 p.m. on the Sunday evening. He gauged the boat and when he had done so she got out. She remarked on the condition of the men who were all *"in liquor, Owen in particular"*. She then walked against the battlements of the bridge and Owen went to her and asked why she did not go with him through the town. She then walked away from him and under the bridge. The two other prisoners were there at the time. The boat left at ten minutes past eight with Christina still walking along the towpath.

John Tansley testified that he saw the woman at the lock-keeper's cottage at Aston Lock, just outside Stone, and she was sharpening a penknife on some steps. When the boat arrived one of the crew shouted abuse at her trying to get her to join the barge. Unfortunately she had no choice and got back on. Owen was seen to offer her a drink which she refused.

A little further along the canal, nearer Sandon than Aston Lock, Thomas Brewer, captain of a boat called *Emma* met Owen's barge. He said that it was getting dusk, near nine o'clock. He asked Owen to get on his boat and have a glass of ale. However, instead of Owen Thomas got on board. He noticed a woman in Owen's boat and said to her, *"How do you do?"* Owen then said to him, pointing at the woman, *"Will you have any of this?"* but he said, *"No."* Thomas then said, *"Jemmy* (meaning Owen) *had concerns with her, and he would that night or they'd burk her."* Thomas then went on board his own boat.

> *"Burk her" probably was a reference to Burk and Hare, the Scottish grave robbers, who not only dug up corpses, but also killed victims to get money for those bodies. Brewer explained to the court that it had become a common expression amongst ordinary people for a method of disposing of a corpse or someone who was in the way.*

Robert Walker, captain of another boat on the canal on June 16th, said that he met a woman on the towpath near Salt Bridge at about ten o'clock and afterwards met one of Pickford's boats. Someone on board said, *"Did you meet a passenger of ours?"* He said that he had and then heard one of the men say in vulgar terms what he wanted to do with her.

Mrs. Ann Mills, lock-keeper at Hoo Mill, told the court that at about twelve o'clock on the Sunday night of June 16th she heard a cry and got up from her bed and saw a woman on the top of a boat in the lock. It was a Pickford boat and there were three men with it. The woman got off the boat and cried for her shoes. After she got her shoes she sat outside the cabin with her legs dangling down. The woman said, *"Don't attempt me. I'll not go into the cabin. I'll not go down there."* The witness then asked one of the men who they had got there and he said they had got a passenger. The witness then asked if anyone was with her and the man answered that her husband was.

James Mills, husband of the last witness, said that he also heard screams, like cries of someone in distress. He saw a woman on top of the cabin and heard his wife question the crew.

William Hatton said that last June he belonged to the boat of Messrs. Bach & Co. and met Owen and Dobell (Thomas) at a watering place between Brindley Bank and Rugeley. They were on the bank and they said, *"Have you seen a woman?"* He said that he had not and they asked again, *"Not between here and the Turnover Bridge?"* He again said that he had not and then they had some talk together which he did not hear. He passed through Hoo Mill Lock between twelve and one o'clock. His boat was going the same way as the Pickford one, but had not come up with it until about a mile after the lock.

When questioned by Mr. Godson for the Defence he said that the canal in some places between Brindley Bank and Rugeley Wharf was about forty feet wide, but shallow at the sides. The Pickford boat when he met Owen and Dobell would have been going at the ordinary rate of speed and about a mile in front of him. Owen and Dobell were coming away from the boat when he met them.

William Lowe was steering a boat near Rugeley on June 17th and heading towards Stoke when he met one of Pickford's boats at about two o'clock in the morning. There was no driver with the boat. He also saw Bach's boat and noticed one man talking to Bach's driver and two men following, one of them without a coat.

James Wilday was captain of a Bach's boat and said that when he was near Handsacre he got up between three and four o'clock and saw a Pickford boat. He saw James Owen jump off and stand upon the middle plank of the boat and wait for the stern end of the boat to come to him. The boy Musson was steering and the witness said to him, *"Hallo, boy, tell your master to look out."* The lad closed the cabin door and if he had not done so the witness could have seen into the cabin.

When questioned by Mr. Godson James said that there was a sharp turn at Brindley Bank and a person unused to a boat might, if the horse jerked, be thrown off. The boat was about thirty feet long and the canal about forty feet wide. Asked by the judge about the canal James said when turning the corner at Brindley Bank he and his crew had had some difficulty in keeping upright. It required care and attention in managing the boat at that place.

The next person to give evidence was young William Musson. He told the court that he got off the boat at Colwich Lock to go to the horse. At that time the woman was in the cabin with her shoes and bonnet off, but when they got to Brindley Bank she was not there. Owen was steering and at that time they had got round the turn as usual. When they got to the stop place he got back onto the boat and asked where the woman was. Owen told him that he thought she was drowned and asked for some silver to pay Dobell. Shortly after he went over the cabin and saw Owen in the hold and a box opened. The woman's two boxes had been tied up with a light coloured cord. He said that he also remembered Bach's boatman calling out to him and Owen telling him to shut the cabin door at that time. As to when he was confined in gaol with the prisoners he did not hear Dobell or Lambert say anything about the woman or the boat.

Under questioning he stated that when he went on board at Brindley Bank Ellis was asleep as he heard him snore. The last time he saw the woman was at Colwich

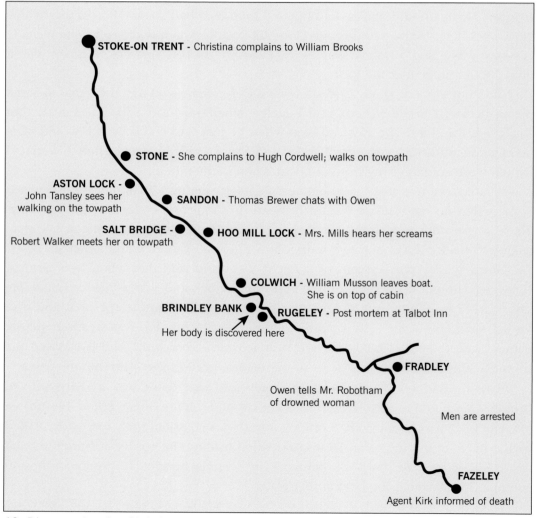

40. Diagram showing Christina's journey.

Lock when she was on the cross bed in the cabin. When the boat was at Aston Lock Thomas said that he *"wished the woman had been at Hell or somewhere else for he hated the sight of her"*. Asked about the incident at Hoo Lock Musson said that he was asleep and did not hear any screams.

The next witnesses were those who were concerned with the crew's actions after Christina had "disappeared". The first of them was John Bladon, wharfinger (person in charge) at Rugeley Wharf. He stated that on the morning of June 17th none of the prisoners came to him to give him information of the incident which they should have done. He went with a man named Johnson to Brindley Bank opposite the towpath to examine the scene. There was a steep bank there ten to fifteen feet above the canal which was about thirty four feet wide and about three feet nine deep.

Ann Lee, wife of Jonathan Lee, landlord of the Wood End, said that at about half past one on June 17th Owen came to her and said that he was afraid they had a woman who had drowned. He could not think what had become of her. She was like one deranged. She had at one time been in the canal up to her knees and he had had great trouble in getting her out. When questioned Mrs. Lee said that Owen seemed *"a little intoxicated, confused from liquor"*. He appeared to tremble, but she was not sure it was from the drink. He had told her that the woman had gone a little walk and kept on repeating *"Collins. Collins."*

Charles Robotham lived at Fradley and was a clerk for the Pickford Company. He said that on the Monday morning June 17th at about six o'clock Owen came and said a bad job had happened. He thought that a woman passenger had drowned herself and she had attempted it before. Owen said that the last he saw of the woman was at Colwich Lock. Owen also told him that he thought the woman was off her head as she kept on calling out *"Collins"*. Owen also told him about the woman's boxes and he, the witness, said that he wanted to have them as they would show the woman's identity. Dobell who was also present said that it was no use having the boxes. He then advised Owen to go back along the canal and look for the woman, but he was unwilling to do so. Having finished questioning the crew he went ahead to see Mr. Kirk, the agent at Fazeley, arriving before the boat. They were both on the wharf side when it arrived and told the crew to come in and bring the load note.

When questioned by the court Robotham said that he went with the constable and searched the cabin where they found the woman's shoes and bonnet. After seeing the state of the cabin he told Owen that it was no place for passengers. Owen said that she had spent the greatest part of the journey in there, but the other two prisoners said that she had not as they would not have her in there. Asked by Sergeant Ludlow about the boxes he said that when he saw them they were both corded. When asked about the men's stay in the lock-up awaiting removal to gaol Robotham said that he heard Owen arguing with the other two and heard him say that he was innocent and burst out crying.

William Kirk said that when the boat arrived at Fazeley he told Lambert to bring the papers into his office and he wanted to speak to him. Lambert's reply was, *"Damn and ----- the woman! If she has drowned herself I cannot help it!"* At that point the witness had said nothing about the disappearance of the woman. Owen was still in the cabin and so the witness told him to come into the office with the papers which he did. Owen said he was sorry, but he had lost a passenger. Owen then said that she had left the boat at Colwich Lock saying she would go no further. Dobell, on coming into the office, said he hoped the woman, *"using a very coarse expression"*, was burning in Hell. At that point the witness went to search for the boxes.

When asked by the court if Dobell had been seen by Mr. Robotham Kirk said that he did not know as he (Dobell) had been in a public house nearby and was "very drunk".

William Harrison, the headborough (constable chosen by the local people) of Fazeley, stated that he was at the canal as the boat arrived. Before anyone had asked any questions Lambert had said, *"D--- and b---- the woman, what do we know about the woman. If she had a mind to drown herself she might."* On being asked Owen said that he believed she had drowned herself. However, when the witness had taken him to Rugeley Owen said, *"She wanted very little drowning."* Intrigued by what Owen had said the witness told the court that he had also been to the place where the victim was drowned about a week later and the water was *"shallow, about eighteen or nineteen inches deep"*. He was surprised anyone could drown in it. He then produced the deceased's bonnet which was of faded blue silk and badly crushed.

Francis Jackson said that Owen had been left in his care at Fazeley and was handcuffed to him. A man had come to see Owen and the prisoner had said to him, *"Do you go and tell the two men in the hold to be sure and swear we left the woman at Colwich Lock."* The man came again the next day and said he had told them to which Owen replied, *"Do it again and be sure."*

The next group of witnesses were those who had seen the body of Christina Collins either before or during the post mortem. Thomas Grant, a boatman, said that he was on Brindley Bank at about five o'clock on June 17th and discovered the body

41. Talbot Inn as an antique shop.

of a woman about eighty yards below the turn. The water was about eighteen inches deep and she was face down and had no shoes or bonnet on. John Johnson was with him and he told the court that the water was warm as was the body. The body was about four feet from the side with a high bank above it. He and Thomas Grant got a drag and managed to get the body to the side. It was then taken to the Talbot Inn, Rugeley.

Hannah Phillips said that she saw the body at Rugeley and the woman had on a gown, a white petticoat, a pair of drawers and a handkerchief. The left arm of the gown was a little torn by the sleeve being ripped from it. The body of the gown was also torn as was the neckerchief. Elizabeth Matthews said that she assisted in taking off the clothes of the deceased. She took off the drawers which were in the same state as the exhibit was now. The cut was where she had cut them to get them off, but the fork part of them seemed to be torn.

* It was custom in those days for village ladies to avail themselves to help in laying out a body ready for a post mortem. However, sometimes they were over-zealous and destroyed vital evidence without realising it by cleaning the corpse too thoroughly.

Mr. Barnett, a Rugeley surgeon, stated that he had examined the body and found two small bruises on the right arm below the elbow. The cavities on the right side of the heart were gorged with blood while the others were healthy. There was frothy mucus about the mouth and throat and water in the stomach. Having been in the profession for twenty years in his opinion the cause of death was suffocation by drowning. Under questioning he did say that the symptoms were not decisive of drowning, but were generally recognised as such.

Once again Robert Collins had to testify that he had identified his wife at Rugeley and again explained how she came to be travelling in the barge. Elizabeth Price who lived in Liverpool said that she saw the deceased on June 15th just before she set off and she "was very neat in her person" being a seamstress.

The final witness was Joseph Orgill, the new

42. Grave of Christina Collins.

witness whom Sergeant Ludlow had procured after having the first trial postponed. He was a convicted bigamist who had served time in Stafford Gaol, but had been granted a pardon. It was not made clear whether that the pardon relied on him giving evidence at this trial, but he had shared a cell with Owen during the first trial and could shed light on the dreadful happenings on the canal journey.

He told the court that on the Sunday night during the first trial he had shared a cell with Owen and they had started up a conversation. He began it by saying, *"Mine is a bad job,"* to which Owen replied, *"So is mine. I can't think why they have taken the boy away from the other two. Perhaps he's going to be a witness against us. But it cannot be about the woman. It must be about something else for he does not know anything about her. The other two men committed a rape upon her and mauled her to death. I am free. I'm afraid there will be a hanging job."*

Owen then went on to tell the witness that they had a woman passenger in the boat who was going to London. They had some whiskey in the boat and they all got drunk except the woman. When they were drunk they began to get rough with her. She got off the boat and when they met another boat they asked if they had seen a woman and they said that they had. He had then said to the other boatman that he would ----- her. His boat carried on until they reached the next lockhouse and the woman was there talking to another woman. She was saying that she was afraid to go with them, but eventually she did get back on board.

Owen continued his account by saying that Dobell and Lambert went on with mauling her all the way and they committed rape or rapes. One of them had cut the trousers before they could do it and she had screamed. He himself had tried to do it, but couldn't. He remained in the boat until they got to Colwich Lock where he was called up top. He was loathe to go as he was drunk. The other two men came into the boat and the boy and the woman went out. She got halfway over the side, but they (Dobell and Lambert) got her in the cabin again where they committed another rape.

The witness told the court that at that point he had asked Owen if the woman was dead and he had replied, *"She was completely mauled to death. I tell you she was dead."* Owen said that what made them do it was they knew what they had done. (In reply to a question from the judge Orgill said that Owen never explained what he meant by *"do it"*.) What he did tell him was that the two had quarrelled amongst themselves as they were afraid that the woman would tell.

After the quarrel Dobell came in to steer the boat and took the woman out of the cabin and laid her on the top. Whether she was pushed off or rolled off in going round the turn he could not tell. Dobell was the last to see her and he said that they had made a bad job of it as they had left her shoes and bonnet in the cabin. Nothing then occurred until they reached Fradley Junction where he proposed to leave her things. Meanwhile Dobell had taken a piece of calico from one box and he argued with him. Dobell said they would be alright if he (Owen) should hold his noise.

Owen then said to the witness, *"Did you take notice of the chapter read by the chaplin? There was so much about hanging in it, but I hope they will not hang us, but we shall get off with transportation and then I don't care. We have made a bad job of it altogether. If we had made an alarm at Rugeley nobody would have known, or if we had put her in the hold and then Pickford would have been fined for not having the straw. Had Dobell and Lambert let the woman alone at Colwich Lock she'd have been alive and well enough."*

Mr. Godson then questioned Orgill at length and seemed satisfied when Orgill agreed that Owen had said that the woman was dead before she was put into the water. His argument in his summing up was that if the deceased was dead before she entered the water then she could not possibly have drowned and so the charge against his clients, that of drowning her, was negated and so the case should be dropped. If the jury were not sure that she was dead then they had to ask themselves if all three men drowned her or just one. Finally he asked the jury, could she not simply have fallen into the water herself and died?

Judge Baron Guerney then summed up the evidence for the jury, adding *"however disgusting the case might be"* that should not shroud their judgement as to the actual crime for which they were charged. Instead it should sharpen their thoughts. At that point the jury retired and within half an hour they returned with their verdict. All three men were found GUILTY of murdering Christina Collins.

The judge in his sentencing said, *"There is also too much reason to believe that she was the object of your lust and that you committed murder to prevent the punishment due to that offence. Look not for your pardon in this world. Prepare for ignominious death. It remains only for me to pronounce the sentence of the law, that you be taken to the place from whence you came (gaol) and there be hanged by the neck until you are dead."*

On Saturday April 11th, 1840 the three men were being prepared for execution when William Ellis (Lambert) was told that he had been given respite from the death penalty and his sentence had been commuted to fourteen years transportation to Australia. (Young Musson's story of Ellis being asleep probably had saved his day.) Ellis asked to see the other two men and his request was granted. Having taken his leave of them Owen and Thomas were led to their place of execution outside Stafford Gaol and were hanged before a crowd of some 10,000 onlookers.

Before Owen and Thomas were cut down Ellis was shown from a distance the suspended bodies of his wretched companions. He was much affected by the awful spectacle.

The bodies, as usual, were placed in the graves without ceremony, *"unshrouded and uncoffined"*. The melancholy spot is railed out and kept with the same neatness which is observable throughout the whole of this well regulated prison.In that enclosure now lie the bodies of five murderers; that being the number executed since the act came into operation which decrees that the bodies *"shall be buried within the precincts of the prison".* The graves are in a row and occupy the entire width of the burial ground. Against the wall, at the head of the graves, on stone slabs are perpetuated the names of the murderers. The inscriptions, white letters on a black background, are as follows:-

ANN WYCHERLEY,
aged 28
Executed for Murder, 5th, May, 1838.

RICHARD TOMLINSON,
aged 22
Executed for Murder, 19th, March, 1834.

MARY SMITH,
aged 24
Executed for Murder, 19th, March, 1834.

JAMES OWEN
aged 39
Executed for Murder, 11th. April, 1840.

GEORGE THOMAS
aged 27
Executed for Murder, 11th, April, 1840.

Room is left in the graveyard for many more graves.

Historical note:- Christina Collins was buried in St. Augustine's Churchyard, Rugeley in June, 1839 and local people subscribed to buy her a decent headstone which still stands today.

43. St. Augustine's Church today.

DYING TO LOVE
Pye Green, Hightown and Burntwood

Love is that strange emotion which is difficult to explain. Why does our heart leap uncontrollably when that one person enters the room? Why do we feel sick and at the same time exhilarated? Many writers have attempted to put into words the anxiety, warmth and tenderness everyone experiences at some times in their lives. Others, like Shakespeare, have shown that love can also be so overwhelming that it can even be destructive as in the sad case of Romeo and Juliet. Surprisingly the following cases may fall into that category.

Florence May Nickless, a 19 year old domestic servant who lived with her parents at 411 Pye Green Road, had fallen helplessly in love with Frederick Smith, a 21 year old colliery horse driver also living in Pye Green Road. On Thursday morning, April 30th 1925, their two bodies were discovered in the canal at Park Bridge, Leacroft. At the inquest which followed on Friday May 8th, held at the Council Chamber by Mr. W.W. Morgan, the assembled crowd were to discover the tragic circumstances which led the couple to take such a momentous decision. Both had left letters describing their reasons.

However, before such tragic revelations could be discussed the hearing had to go through the usual court formalities. Thomas Stevens, a boatman of 20 Hatton Street, Bilston, stated that at about 5.45 a.m. on Thursday April 30th he was making his way along the canal close to Park Bridge when he discovered a man's jacket and cap and a woman's hat on the side of the canal. His attention had been drawn to the articles because his horse had shied at them. Sensing that something was amiss he began to feel in the water with his boat hook around where the clothes were lying. Finding nothing at the time he took the clothes to the police station at Cannock Road, Hednesford.

Police Constable Cartledge told the hearing that, acting on the boatman's information, he proceeded with Inspector Dale at about 6.25 a.m. to the place on the canal where the articles had been found. He assisted with dragging operations and at 8.15 a.m. the body of a man was discovered. The drags were then thrown into the water again at the same spot and soon the body of a girl was found. Both people were dead and their corpses rigid. With the exception of the clothes found on the canal side both bodies were fully clothed and the clothing was in no way disarranged. The girl was even wearing a pair of gloves, which still remained buttoned. The bodies were then removed to the mortuary at Cannock.

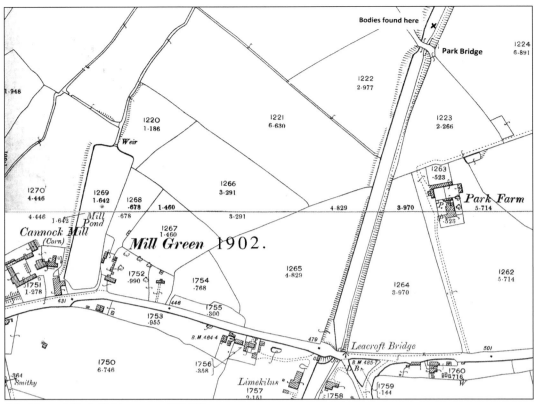

44. Map of Park Bridge area (1902)

The constable then went on to tell the court that the water in the place where the bodies were found was very deep. Bathers used the spot in the summer because it allowed diving without fear of injury. He also said that there were no marks on either body and no sign of any struggle having taken place. On examining the man's jacket he discovered several letters belonging to the man. One of the papers was a Discharge Paper relating to the Territorials and identified the man as Frederick Smith. Another letter, also discovered in the pocket, was from his girlfriend, Florence Nickless. Yet another letter was written to Smith's sister. Those letters were to reveal the tragedy in heartrending detail.

Frances Miriam Jellyman of 10 Brickkiln Street, Brownhills told the hearing that Frederick Smith was her brother. Previous to meeting with an accident to his shoulder four years ago he had been employed as a horse driver at East Cannock Colliery, but afterwards he had been given a very light job at the pit. Unfortunately his arm got worse and he had not been able to work for about the last fifteen weeks. Frances said that that had made him depressed and when she saw him about ten days ago he had said that if he did not get any better then he would do something to himself. Finally she told the court that her brother had been keeping company with Florence Nickless.

Inspector Dale then produced the letter to Frances which had been found in Frederick's pocket and she identified the handwriting as her brother's. Inspector Dale then proceeded to read the letter to the court. It read:-

"Dear Sister, - I do hope you are now on the road to complete recovery, also that this act of mine won't upset you very much. Having told you that I decided to end it all, I do hope it won't hurt you so hard as it would otherwise. Perhaps, dear Mirris, knowing all, you will understand and forgive me. Now I told Florrie, as you know, and asked her to give me up, but she refused. I told her what I was going to do, and she said that if I did she would too. Oh, God knows, how I have tried to persuade her to hang on to life, but it's no use and she is bent on it, so I am saying nothing more. I know that you would do anything for me, but, little sister, (if this is the coward's way out) I should be a much bigger coward to become a burden to anyone. Well, Mirris, I should like you to have my watch and chain and wallet and anything else you want. We are not doing it without considering everything, and we decided over a week ago. Oh, why should I have lived to meet Flo only to bring trouble to her people? We have nine packets of salts of lemon which we shall take between us and if that doesn't do it we shall finish it by drowning. Well, I thing I have said enough so I will close. Hoping you will forgive me. With love from your unfortunate brother, Fred. Goodbye X.

P.S. Enclosed is a photo of Florrie which I ask you to keep.

PPS. Tell Uncle Harry to give you the money if there is anything coming. Goodbye."

* Salts of lemon was a dangerous poison used for cleaning leather, scouring metals like brass and copper and removing stains. It was a mixture of potassium oxalate and cream of tartar. If digested in the right amount it could kill within ten minutes.

Mrs. Hannah Beeston of Pye Green Road told the hearing that Frederick Smith had lodged with her since March, 1921. He had had his accident at the pit about three weeks before moving in, but had not told her of it until some time after being with her. He was, she understood, found a light job at the pit. He resumed work after the coal strike in the spring of 1921, but was forced to give it up after a month or so and was *"at play"* for about nine months. She believed that he had a bone broken in his shoulder and he had had treatment at Birmingham and Wolverhampton hospitals and had been an in-patient at one of the institutions for some time. He had not worked since January 10th last. He had complained to her on several occasions about the dreadful pain in his arm, the muscles of which were gradually wasting away. She also said that he had been very distressed since being discharged from hospital on April 3rd 1925. A fortnight ago he had told her that he was *"fed up"*, though he had never threatened in her presence to do anything or take his own life. It was evident though that his condition was preying on his mind. He went out of her house at about 5.45 p.m. on Wednesday evening and that was the last time that she saw him alive.

When shown the paper, by Inspector Dale, on which three letters were written by Smith Mrs. Beeston said that they had been taken from a writing pad belonging to Smith which he kept at her house. She also said that she had seen him writing a letter on the Wednesday afternoon.

Inspector Dale then produced two more letters which had been found in Smith's pocket. One was in Florence's handwriting and read:-

> *"My dear Mother, - Please forgive me for the misery I am about to cause you, but I am writing this letter to wish you all goodbye. I never guessed that life could be so uninteresting at 19. You already know that Fred had nothing to look forward to in the future, so we have decided that the sooner we leave this world the better. We have both the happy consolation of knowing that we shall soon be reunited with the dear departed. Please, dear mother, don't blame Fred for this, for as God is my witness, I am doing it of my own free will. Fred thinks it is the only way out for him as he does not wish to be a burden to anyone and I feel I should not be doing my duty if I let him go alone. I hope everyone will forgive me for this. With all my love, from your ever loving Florrie.*
>
> *PS. Whatever Lucy (a friend) would like in memory of me, will you please let her have, Florrie."*

Mrs. Nickless, wife of John Nickless a colliery bankman, told the hearing that her daughter Florence had been keeping company with Smith since September, 1924 and in reply to the coroner said that the two seemed "very much attracted to each other". She said that her daughter was a domestic servant, but owing to illness had been at home for the last three months. On Wednesday evening, April 29th, Florence left home at about six o'clock and later the same night her daughter and Smith were seen together in Cannock.

Lucy Bould, Florence's friend, said that she lived with her father at 43 Mill Street, Cannock and knew Florence very well and they had become intimate friends. She also knew that Florence was keeping company with Smith. They had both called at her home in Mill Street on the Wednesday evening, but they then appeared alright and in their usual spirits. When asked by the coroner if she had ever heard either of them threaten to commit suicide, Lucy said, *"Well about a week ago, she (Florrie) told me she had a great secret to tell me if I would not tell anyone. Then she told me that she and Fred had decided to end it together, but I did not think she meant it."*

In summing up the coroner, Mr. Morgan, said that *"it was very evident that the young couple had got into a very sad and depressed state of mind"* and the letters *amply proved that. Smith's unfortunate physical state had rendered him and then his girlfriend unable to see any brightness in the future and that had preyed on their minds. By law the only verdict he could give must be "Suicide by drowning whilst temporarily of unsound mind".*

On Tuesday afternoon, May 12th a large crowd assembled at Cannock Cemetery for the funerals of the unfortunate couple. Reverend Price of Cannock conducted the service which was held in the cemetery chapel and later the couple were buried in separate graves.

The next case is somewhat strange in that it also involves two lovers who discuss suicide, but at the last moment one of them decides not to follow it through. The inquest which followed the death of one saw the verdict of "Wilful Murder" passed on the other – strange you may think. But that was the law!

Elizabeth Kirkham ,22 years old and a native of Hightown, was a domestic servant at Sutton Coldfield. She had met and fallen in love with John William Berkeley Holloway, a 24 year old Royal Marine attached to H.M.S. Queen Elizabeth, Portsmouth. They became engaged and all seemed fine, but on the Saturday evening, September 1st, 1923 tragedy happened. The pair left 17 Tolladine Road where Holloway lived and they had been staying and did not return that evening. The next morning Kirkham appeared at Tolladine Road in a state of great distress and obviously ill, shouting that her fiancée was dead. After the body was found the police discovered various letters which were introduced at the inquest which was held on Tuesday September 4th at Worcester.

Gertrude Roome, daughter of Ebenezer Roome of 17 Tolladine Road, said that Holloway was adopted by her mother when he was fifteen months old. He was engaged to Elizabeth Kirkham and the two had stayed at Tolladine Road since August 7th . The couple had discussed marriage, but had not come to any decision as to a date; it was to be either Christmas or Easter. The two had left the house on the Saturday at about 7.45 p.m. saying that they were going for a walk. They did not return that night, but at about 7.45 a.m. on the Sunday Lizza Kirkham had come running up the path seeming very upset and without her hat or jacket. She had said, *"Come quick, Will is dying."*

The witness then went with her across a field to a spot about 300 or 400 yards from the house. She saw Holloway lying in a ditch and he was dead. Miss Kirkham's sports coat was under his head and another cloth brown coat of Miss Kirkham's was over his legs. Miss Kirkham then lay down by the side of the body and said, *"Will, do come back to me."* When questioned Gertrude said that she had never heard either of them threaten to take their own lives.

Police Constable Dudley said that when he found Holloway he was fully dressed in the uniform of the Marines, except for his cap and a belt which were a short distance away. He said that he found a letter signed by Holloway in the tunic pocket. The letter read:-

"Dear mother and to all at home – I daresay that you are all on thorns over me not going back to my time, but to speak the truth I am rather put out in my mind. I have found no future to look forward to, so that this will find I have gone elsewhere, taking Lizzie with me, so do not think me at all insane. I know what I am doing – With fondest love to all , from your son, Will. Good Bye."

The constable said that he also found another letter in the woman's brown coat. It read:-

"To Miss Kirkham, 13 Platt Street, Hightown, Hednesford, Staffordshire – My dear Alice, - Well dear, you will want to know the reason I am writing like this, but it is to tell you I am tired of my life, so I am putting an end to it tonight, also Will. Do not think hard of me as all's well that ends well. Please see that my sister has all my things, as I leave all I have got to her ....Please forgive me for writing like this, but it is as I feel. Remember me to all friends."

Constable Dudley said that he also found the following prayer in the woman's coat.

"We commend to Thy Fatherly goodness. O Lord, for those we have left at home, our relations and friends, also those who are in any way afflicted in mind, body and estate; give them patience, relieve them of their sufferings, according to their several necessities, that they have the joys of the world, inasmuch as to love, honour and obey; so we may ask this – to the honour of Thy Holy name, Lord. This we beg. Amen."

It was later found to be in Holloway's handwriting.

The constable went on to tell the court that he found a bottle near the body and when searching the house he found yet another letter which read:-

"The one who finds this, - Will you kindly return to Miss Annie Jones, Fairview, Lichfield, Doc Bank, Sutton Coldfield. This is a request from Miss L. Kirkham to Miss Jones. Will you kindly bequeath that all the articles enclosed may be safely handed over to my loving sister, Fanny; also the case that was handed to me as a present from my boy. I hope you will kindly do this as a

last favour for me and oblige me, your loving friend, Lizzie Kirkham. This is my sole wish, so goodbye and the best of luck, from two lovers who find rest a pleasant future. Miss Elizabeth Kirkham, late of Oakengates, Lichfield Road, Sutton Coldfield."

Elizabeth Kirkham, after being cautioned by the coroner, then gave evidence. She stated that she was engaged to Holloway and on the Saturday she had purchased some salts of lemon in Worcester to clean his white hat. On the Saturday evening he offered her something from the bottle which he had already drunk from, but she refused it. However, he forced it between her teeth, but she managed not to take much. Then both of them were in pain. He grasped her by the throat and tried to strangle her. She then blacked out and did not remember any more. She also told the hearing that he had threatened her the night before in front of his mother and on that Friday night he had caught her by the throat and tried to strangle her in front of everyone.

When questioned by the coroner about the letter which she had written she said that Holloway had forced her to write it and she had no idea that he was planning for them both to die. As for the salts of lemon she said that she thought it was for the grease on his hat. When shown the letter to Miss Jones Elizabeth replied, *"That is not my writing. I know nothing whatever about it. It is not Holloway's writing."* Asked about the prayer she said, *"The boy (Holloway) sent me that when he was at sea. I have always carried that prayer with me at the back of my purse. Neither of us has parents."*

At the end of the hearing the jury stated that they came to the conclusion that the pair had intended to take their own lives. The coroner then said that their verdict meant that Kirkham should receive a verdict of "Wilful Murder". When questioned by the jury as to his decision he said, *"Unfortunately that is the interpretation of the law"* and so Elizabeth Kirkham was arrested for the murder of Holloway.

On Tuesday October 23rd, 1923 Elizabeth Kirkham appeared at Worcester Assizes before Mr. Justice Shearman charged with the murder of her sweetheart, John William Berkeley Holloway. Mr. Powell for the Prosecution told the jury that it was not an ordinary case of murder. The jury might have heard of "suicide pacts", but the law was that if two people agreed to commit suicide and one survived then the survivor was guilty of murder. After that he went through all the evidence from the inquest, pointing out the possibilities of a pact. Did she buy the salts of lemon as a poison for each of them to take? Had they gone into the field to commit suicide? What of the letters written supposedly by both parties? The jury would have to decide.

Inspector Mills said that when the prisoner was charged she said, *"What? Charging me with murder! He forced the bottle into my mouth and also tried to strangle me."*

Under questioning Elizabeth stated that she was going to marry Holloway at Christmas, but she did not intend to help him kill himself. On the Friday night he had thrown her between two chairs and caught her by the throat. As to the letter she wrote she again said that he had forced her to write it – *"he caught my hand and told me what to put in it"*, but she did not want to write it. As to the taking of the poison she again stated that he took some first and then tried to force it between her lips, but she became unconscious. Finally she was vehement that she would not have gone out with Holloway if she had thought that he was going to commit suicide. After intense questioning Elizabeth collapsed and had to be assisted back to the dock where she received medical aid.

Having heard all the evidence the jury returned a verdict of NOT GUILTY. There was some applause in the gallery which the judge quickly stopped. However, he added that he fully agreed with the jury's verdict and when the Crown offered no evidence on the charge of attempted suicide Elizabeth Kirkham was discharged.

The final case in this trilogy of love is perhaps the one that most readers are familiar with – that of unrequited love, lies and deceit. One partner, usually the female, is deeply in love, whilst their opposite number is in the relationship for what they can get. It can only end in heartache and tragically, as in our case, with the death of the one whose love has been rejected.

Twenty one year old Jennie Ross of 6 Blue Ball Row, Burntwood had met and fallen madly in love with Albert Victor (nicknamed Champ), a twenty six year old who came from Balsall Heath, Birmingham. Outwardly their relationship seemed fine; Champ had even come to live with Jennie and her parents, Phoebe and Harry, and the two had spoken of marriage which was supposed to take place on January 2nd, 1930. It was then to everyone's surprise that Jennie went missing on Saturday December 14th, 1929. Despite the efforts of the family and local police she was not found until January 16th when her lifeless corpse was discovered floating in the canal at Brownhills.

The inquest which began on January 26th, 1930 in front of the coroner, Mr. F.W. Cooper, at Brownhills revealed the shocking, one-sided relationship between Jennie and Albert. Because the case had created so much local interest it was decided that the jury should be made up of local men, with Mr. Jonah Deakin as the foreman.

The first witness was Dr. R. O. Bradford who said that he had made two examinations of the corpse and Mr. Dyke, a pathologist, had assisted him with the second examination. Both men were convinced that there were no signs of violence on the body and no evidence of disease, injury or poisoning. They had found a fracture of the ribs from the sixth to the eleventh, but those injuries were sustained after death, probably caused by her being caught between canal boats. Strangely, there was no evidence either of drowning and that was why Dr. Bradford

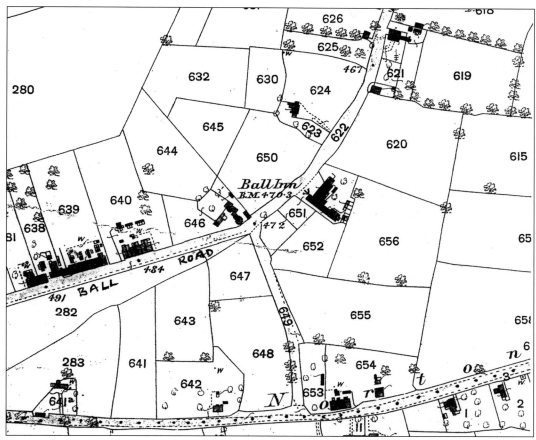

45. Map of the Ball Inn area, Burntwood, 1882.

had asked for the assistance of Mr. Dyke in the second post mortem. They both eventually concluded that it was reasonable to suppose that her death had been due to drowning even though the usual signs were not there. (A person drowns because the lungs fill with water.) Mr. Dyke stated that in all his career he had never met a case of drowning which hadn't displayed the classic signs. The only possible explanation was that because it had happened in December the extreme cold of the water could have caused Jennie to die from asphyxia or shock.

The coroner had one final question for the doctors and that was whether there were any signs that Jennie was in a "certain condition" to which they replied that she was not. All would become clear later.

Harry Ross was next to give evidence. He told the hearing that his daughter and Champ were to be married in the January and because of that he had allowed Champ to live with them. However, he had failed to pay his keep and so had been asked to leave. He had returned to Birmingham which made Jennie very upset, so much so that on one occasion she had remarked to her father that she had *a good mind to make a hole in the water*" as she was so unhappy. He had thought nothing

46. Picture of the Blue Ball Inn. The Ball Inn could have been built as early as 1780, but was definitely there from 1825. It stood in Ball Road, today's Chase Road, Burntwood.

of that at the time, but when she went missing, fearing that she had done it, he organised a search of the local waters and sent his son, also Harry, to Birmingham to find and question Champ.

Harry Ross, junior, told the court that he had met Champ in Birmingham on Sunday December 15th, the day after Jennie had disappeared, and had asked him about Jennie's whereabouts , but, as he told the court, Champ *"did not seem to care whether Jennie had been home or not"*. Harry also told the hearing that he had heard his sister threaten to kill herself on several occasions.

Mabel Podmore of Hammerwich, Jennie's sister, told the court that Jennie had intimated to her that she was pregnant by Champ and she had no reason to disbelieve her. Jennie had told her that Champ had had to leave her father's house because he had not paid board for two weeks. She had said that he was supposed to get work in Tamworth in the November but had not. After he had gone back to Birmingham he had sent Jennie a letter which Jennie had shown the witness. It had said,

"I have come back home; is it all off with us? Don't say so. Let your mother keep my things until I give her money."

Mabel told the hearing that the letter made her sister very upset and it was then that she had made the water threats.

After receiving the letter Jennie had gone off to Birmingham to see Champ and had persuaded him to come back to Hammerwich. He had done so and had stayed two weeks, each day going out to work at Brownhills, or so they believed. Her sister had gone to Brownhills to meet him on one occasion, but he had not turned up. He had left Mabel's home on December 14th and her sister had once more gone to Brownhills to meet him, but once again he had not turned up. Jennie came back to Hammerwich and waited in the witness's house until 7.30 p.m. and then had left saying that she was going home. At 9.50 p.m. another sister came to the witness's home to see if Jennie was still there as she had not returned home. On the Sunday she saw Champ at her mother's home. Her brother had persuaded him to come.

It was then time for Albert Victor to give evidence. He told the hearing that he had first met Jennie at a public house called The Littleton Arms where she worked as a barmaid with his mother. The two had become friendly and had started going out together. She had told him that she was in a "certain condition" and that she had told her family. Asked by the coroner whether he believed her or not he replied that he no reason not to believe her.

He then went on to tell the court that everything he had told everyone about Brownhills and work was a lie. To keep up the lie he had actually gone out to "work" each day, but had spent the whole time just wandering around the area and that was why he had failed to meet Jennie on several occasions. The same was true about the job in Tamworth – he had never tried to find work there. When questioned about whether Jennie had ever spoken of suicide to him he replied that she had only once said that she was fed up with being at home.

Not that Champ needed an alibi as there was no suggestion of foul play, but the final witness was Albert's father who said that his son had arrived at his home at about 5.30 p.m. on the evening of Saturday 14th and had stayed until 9.30 a.m. the following morning. He had slept with his brother, George.

After the coroner had summed up the evidence it did not take the jury long to come to their verdict – suicide whilst the state of mind was unbalanced due to the circumstances of living at home and the desertion by her boyfriend. The coroner obviously agreed, but had some rather unsavoury words for Albert Victor – *"I assume you have a conscience? You acted the part of a coward in twice running away instead of explaining things to Jennie. I my estimation you are a moral coward."*

With the comments of the coroner still fresh I leave the readers to make up their own minds on the character of Albert Victor.

REAL WHO DUNNITS
Bridgtown - Pye Green

The Victorians laid great stress on what they termed "deathbed confessions" presuming that the dying person would not want to go to his or her grave committing yet another sin and so any such confessions were taken very seriously. There are a number of cases during the nineteenth century when crimes, which had baffled the police, suddenly were explained when the perpetrator lay on his or her deathbed. Was the following the same or just the last rantings of a tortured soul?

On October 13th, 1890 a reporter from the *Cannock Advertiser* was sent to Bridgtown to interview several witnesses who had been with Jeremiah Poyner of North Street when he lay dying. Apparently he had confessed to the murder of a young girl named Morris some six and a half years earlier. The rumour had spread around the district quickly and so the reporter wanted to see if there was any truth in it.

On that Monday he interviewed two men who were supposed to have been at Jeremiah's side when he passed away. Unfortunately the interview did not go as he wished because both men were reluctant to believe the confession. However, the paper decided to print the statements which were as follows:-

"Mr. ------, I hear that Jeremiah Poyner, before dying, made a confession to you that he had murdered the girl who was found in the clay hole some six and a half years ago?"

"Sir, it is all wrong. He never made any confession to me."

"Well, it is rumoured that he did confess and that you were the one he confessed to."

"Yes, I know it is, and I only wish I could find the one who first stated that I said he had confessed. I would bring them to justice."

"Certainly," answered our representative, *"if there is no truth in the statement the one who invented it ought to be punished. I came to you in order that I may learn the truth, and if you wish I will contradict the rumour, at least as far as you are implicated."*

"There is no truth in it at all. I was sent for to Poyner on the Monday night, but it was only to help hold him as he was raving and unmanageable. He never made any confession; and if he had I should not have taken any notice as the man was not accountable for what he did say. The only thing on his mind seemed his anxiety to be at work and it was with great difficulty that he was kept in bed."

At that point, realising he was going to get no further, the reporter left Bridgtown, but the rumours persisted and so the paper reviewed the inquest into the death of the girl. That inquest had taken place on Tuesday February 5th, 1884 before the coroner, Mr. Morgan. It stated that a girl named Ellen Morris, not quite fourteen, had been employed by Mrs. Emily Hughes at the Royal Exchange, Watling Street in Bridgtown as a domestic servant. On Friday February 1st, 1884 she had been sent by Mrs. Hughes to the Post Office to purchase some flannel. However, she had not returned and so a search was instigated and finally her body was discovered on the Sunday morning in a nearby clay hole called Brickyard Pool on the corner of Watling Street and Bridge Street.

The first person to give evidence was Robert Morris, brother of the deceased, who had identified the body. He said that Ellen was thirteen years of age last April and had been employed by Mrs. Hughes at the Royal Exchange public house. He had last seen her alive just a few days before the Friday and had asked her how she was getting on in her job. She said that she was *"comfortable"* and happy. Robert told the hearing that he had no reason to think that she took her own life.

Mrs. Hughes, wife of Benjamin Hughes, landlord of the Royal Exchange, said that the girl had been employed by her for four months and one week. Ellen was nearly fourteen and a *"big, fine girl"*; in fact her size made her look older. At about a quarter to eight on the Friday evening she had sent Ellen to buy the flannel from the Post Office. It was rather a rough night and rained a little. Ellen did not return and she and her husband could find nothing out about her that night. They had thought that the girl might have decided to head for home in Walsall where her mother lived. The

47. The Royal Exchange, Bridgtown.

next morning, anxious about Ellen, they sent to the Post Office to make enquiries about the girl and when they found out that she had been there and had purchased the flannel they decided to inform the police.

Mrs. Hughes went on to tell the hearing that Ellen had never been missing from the public house at night since she had been employed there - *"She was a very good girl and we had no complaints to make against her when her age was taken into consideration. She was always well in health and generally full of spirits."* Also Mrs. Hughes said, *"She has never been strange in her manner. Ellen had said to her children sometimes when they were having a meal together that it would be the last time they would eat together, but by that she meant that the children should behave at meals otherwise she would not eat with them."* Whenever she went to the Post Office she always went the way of the brickyard pit and, because it was thought to be dangerous, she had been warned not to go that way. However, all Ellen would say was that she preferred to go that way. Finally, Mrs. Hughes told the inquest that in her opinion Ellen had accidentally fallen into the water and drowned.

Another witness, Joseph Fuller, a miner living in Broad Street, Bridgtown, said that he met the girl between the Royal Exchange and the brickyard pool at about five minutes to eight on the Friday evening. He was walking along the footpath and was about 40 yards from the Royal Exchange when he met the deceased heading towards the inn which would be about half way between the inn and where she was found. He said that he knew who it was because he was carrying his lantern and it shone on her. She said *"Good night"* to him and he replied, *"Hallo, is that you? Goodnight."* He was sure the girl was going in the direction of the Exchange at the time, but must have gone back towards the pit.

Police Constable Armstrong testified that he had been informed of the girl's disappearance at nine o'clock on the Saturday morning by Mr. Hughes's son. He then began to make enquiries and sent a message to her home in Walsall. On the Sunday morning Robert Morris arrived to say that she had not gone home. He left, but soon after returned with the girl's hat which he said he had just found floating in Brickyard Pool. P.C. Armstrong and others then helped in dragging the pool and after a while they found the girl's body. When they examined the body they found no marks of violence. When questioned by the coroner the constable said that there was *"no suspicion of foul play"*. He did, however, remark that *"there was no rail by the pool and no protection whatever"*.

At that point there was some discussion regarding the safety of the pool area. It was stated that as early as 1881 it had been drawn to the attention of the Local Board and again in 1882. As a consequence Mr. Anderson, the owner, had been requested to fence it, but he had failed to do so and the Board, though annoyed with him, had not insisted. Mr. Haydn Whitehouse, one of the jury, produced a copy of a letter, complaining about the pool, which he had sent to the Board in 1882.

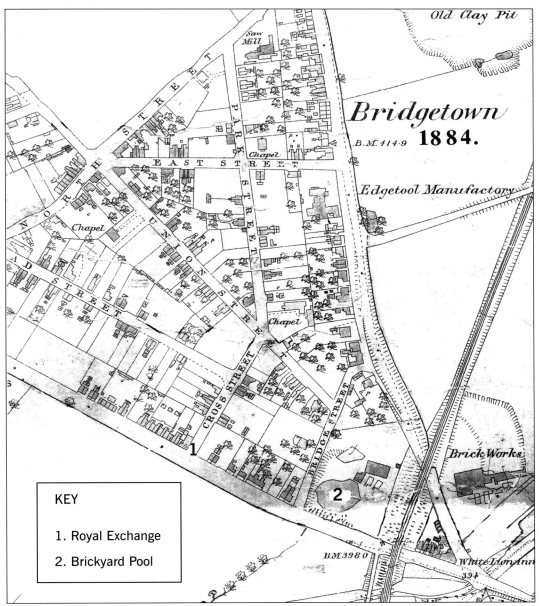

48. Map of Bridgtown

There were other witnesses at the inquest who said that the Friday evening was stormy and it could be that the girl's hat had blown into the water and in the effort to retrieve it she had fallen in and drowned.

Mr. Morgan, the coroner, in summing up said that there was no evidence whatsoever to suggest that the girl had committed suicide, quite the contrary. He thought it highly probable that the suggested theory that the deceased's hat might have been blown off by the wind and carried in the direction of the pool and following it she might have toppled over into the water and met her death was likely.

The jury thought likewise and returned a verdict of "Found Drowned", but desired the coroner to write to the Local Board to say that as far as the jury were concerned the Board was to blame for not taking measures to have the pool fenced in.

Strangely no one at the inquest or in the police force queried the absence of the flannel which Ellen had definitely bought. Of course it may have sunk with the girl, but that seems unlikely as when she fell in she would naturally have struggled for her life and in doing so would have let go of it. It then, like her hat, would have floated away from the corpse and to the surface. It may seem almost irrelevant, but in those days robbery or murder had been committed for less than a piece of flannel. Suicide could also be ruled out as she would surely not have gone and bought the flannel beforehand.

As the reporter wrote, *"The case seems enshrouded in mystery and we suppose it must still remain so."*

*The Morris family of Walsall suffered an horrendous two years between 1883 and 1884. In 1883 Ellen's father had been accidentally killed on Quinton's Hill and just after Ellen's sad death her sister was found dead in bed.

The next episode involves Cannock Chase itself. With the vast acreage of Cannock Chase on our doorstep do you wonder just how many times it may just have been used as a cemetery? People have for years been scattering the ashes of their loved ones there in some favourite spot while others in a sorry state of mental suffering have used the Chase to end their torment. But have other more evil people been discarding corpses of their victims there to avoid detection? Is the following case just the tip of a rather gruesome iceberg?

On Wednesday November 26th, 1941 Rose Ellen Jones of 19 Brindley Village, Hednesford and her two friends, Mary Ford and Kathleen Derry, also of Brindley Village, were pruning trees in Badger's Hill Plantation, Pottal Pool when they discovered a skull and bones at the foot of a tree. They gathered them together and then reported their find to Mr. Tribe, the forester, who immediately informed the police. Police Constable Taylor arrived at the scene and had the bones transferred to the mortuary for examination.

At the subsequent inquest on the following Monday, conducted by Mr. W.W. Morgan, the three girls gave their evidence of finding the bones followed by P.C. Taylor. He told the hearing that the plantation was planted in 1921 and was weeded up until 1925, but from them until May, 1940 it had not been touched. It was then thinned out and was again being thinned when the discovery was made. He said that the bones were found in the forest on the right hand side going from Pottal Pool to Broadhurst Green and were about fifty yards inside the wood and about a quarter of a mile from the nearest road. A careful search was made of the area for a week and the ground was forked up for a distance of about twenty square yards and other bones were located.

When asked by the coroner if the corpse could have been there for years P.C. Taylor said that it could. He also added that no sign of a struggle was found nor was any clothing or flesh on the bones. The exact place where they were found was very thick undergrowth and comprised of bracken, moss, fir cones and needles. The constable said that Sergeant Ward and Detective Constable Littlewood had also taken part in the investigation and every possible enquiry had been made, including those through Scotland Yard. Details of the corpse had been sent throughout the country, but the identity of the body had not been discovered.

In reply to Superintendent Brooks Taylor said that the bones were scattered and were a quarter of a mile from Wishing Stone Lane. The quickest way of getting to the place was through one of the "rides" (large gaps cut through the dense plantation to allow access for vehicles and act as breaks to slow down forest fires). The remains were an equal distance between two of those rides. The foreman of the jury told the hearing that there had been a big fire on that side of the plantation and that those rides were cut during the last sixteen years.

The only other witness was Dr. Webster, Director of the Home Office Laboratory. He stated that he had made a detailed examination of the bones and had found no muscle or flesh. Moss had grown on some of the bones, but he was positive that the skull was that of a female. There was a small depressed fracture at the back of the skull which, he was certain, had been inflicted before death. There was also a small indentation in another part, surrounded by a red stain and he was of the opinion that the woman had received a blow on the front of the head which had caused her to fall backwards on to some object, thereby causing the depression on the back of the skull.

In reply to the coroner he said that the woman was about fifty years of age and using well known calculations she was about fifty nine to sixty inches tall. He was certain that she had met her death by violence, causing a fracture of the skull and inter-cranial haemorrhage. In his opinion the bones had been in the forest for at least two and a half years, but might be as long as seven. What he found extraordinary was the lack of shoes which would have survived and so he thought that the body was stripped and left naked. In all his investigations he had never known shoes to completely disappear.

Another thing that he found extraordinary was that there was no trace of clothing at all. In another case that he had investigated where a woman had been buried for ten years there had still been traces of clothing. At that point one juryman asked if it had ever been established how long it took for clothing to completely disappear to which Webster replied that it depended on the type of clothing and weather conditions, but he could only use his experience. In another case he had investigated only weeks before the clothing had been buried beneath a manure heap, a place where you would have expected the organic matter to have helped in disposal, but some of the clothing had still remained after ten years. That had been proved by the murderer's confession of when he buried his victim.

Superintendent Brooks then asked about the possibility of false teeth, because there were no teeth found in the skull, to which Webster replied that he did not think that the woman had them because they usually left a narrowing of the gums and bones beneath and prevented the look that elderly people usually had who had no false teeth. The absence of the false teeth might indicate that the woman was of rather low class as ordinary class people usually wore teeth. The coroner interrupted there saying, *"Some don't bother to get used to false teeth,"* to which Webster replied that he agreed. However, the woman did have one tooth left, the rest being taken out during her lifetime. She had also suffered from pyorrhoea (a gum disease). Finally Dr. Webster said that there were signs that the woman had had children.

Questioned as to the possibility of foxes having scattered the bones because there was a lair nearby, Dr. Webster said that a fox would not touch rotten human flesh and also there were no teeth marks on the bones to suggested predation by animals. Foxes may have pulled the bones apart thereby scattering them. When asked if the body could have been dismembered he stated that there were no cutting signs anywhere – the skeleton had merely come apart itself through putrefaction.

The coroner then closed the inquest saying that the woman met her death by violence and it was in the interests of justice that every enquiry should be made to identify the body and bring to justice the murderer. Dr. Webster told the coroner that he advised that the bones be kept and Superintendent Brooks said that he intended to hand all of them to Birmingham Laboratory to be stored there.

The identity of the woman has never been discovered and I presume the bones are still at Birmingham.

LIST OF SOURCES

1. Newspapers:-

    Aris's Birmingham Gazette

    Cannock Advertiser

    Lichfield Mercury

    Staffordshire Advertiser

    Wolverhampton Chronicle

2. Maps:-

    Ordnance Survey Maps of Cannock area – 1884 and 1902 housed at Cannock Library.

    Ordnance Survey Maps of Burntwood and Chasetown areas housed at Lichfield Library.

    Various other Ordnance Survey Maps housed at Stafford County Archives.

3. Census information:- Years 1841 to 1901 at Cannock Library.

4. St. Luke's Birth, Death and Marriage Records at Cannock Library.

5. 1914 Blue Book.

6. Books:-

    The Rugeley Poisoner – Dave Lewis

    Sinner, Saint or Political Pawn – Kathleen Smith

    Police Experiences – Thomas Woollaston